ALONE AFTER SCHOOL
A Self-Care Guide for Latchkey
Children and Their Parents

Helen L. Swan
and
Victoria Houston

Prentice-Hall, Inc.   Englewood Cliffs, New Jersey

Prentice-Hall International, Inc., *London*
Prentice-Hall of Australia, Pty. Ltd., *Sydney*
Prentice-Hall Canada, Inc., *Toronto*
Prentice-Hall of India Private Ltd., *New Delhi*
Prentice-Hall of Japan, Inc., *Tokyo*
Prentice-Hall of Southeast Asia Pte. Ltd., *Singapore*
Whitehall Books, Ltd., Wellington, *New Zealand*
Editora Prentice-Hall do Brasil Ltda., *Rio de Janeiro*
Prentice-Hall Hispanoamericana, S.A., *Mexico*

© 1985 *by*

Helen L. Swan and Victoria Houston

Library of Congress Cataloging in Publication Data

Swan, Helen L.,
  Alone after school.

  Bibliography: p.
  Includes index.
  1. Latchkey children—Handbooks, manuals, etc.
I. Houston, Victoria,   II. Title.
HQ777.65.S93   1985   640'.24054   85-3442

ISBN 0-13-023011-1

ISBN 0-13-023003-0 {PBK}

Printed in the United States of America

For Rob, Andrea, Nicole, Steve, and Ryan

The authors wish to acknowledge the expert assistance of Dr. Barton D. Schmitt and Judith M. Cooke.

FOREWORD

People who care about the welfare of American children can sleep a little better knowing that *Alone After School* is available to parents and children. Helen Swan and Victoria Houston strike a good balance in their book, asserting that children *need* adult supervision, while recognizing the realities of work and family in America. In the cultural and economic environment we face, most parents of school-age children are employed outside the home, and that translates into millions of "latchkey" or "self-care" children. As I see it, the risks to these children are four: (1) that the child will feel bad — bored, afraid, or rejected; (2) that the child will act badly — be a nuisance in the neighborhood or in the family; (3) that the child will be treated badly — by older children, adults, or other family members (and this includes all forms of abuse); and (4) that the child will develop badly — growing up too quickly or missing out on important experiences.

I think a family armed with *Alone After School* can do much to overcome all four risks. That's a big step. Some people speak of the positive aspects of self-care — encouraging responsibility, for example — but few of us would go out of our way to establish the need for self-care. Most families see self-care as a necessary part of an overall economic plan, adaptation to need.

Any family that honestly and sensitively uses this book will find that it has some built-in fail-safe features. For example, doing the exercises and reading the text make it clear that self-care is *not* for very young children (any parent who thinks "how could my eight-year-old understand all this!" is being sent a signal). Of the nearly forty children cited as examples in the book, almost all are at least nine years old (— and most are older). Of course, no one can give an exact age cutoff suitable for all children and situations, but the general rule is "older is better." Amen to that. If a child *is* ready for self-care, *Alone After School* will help make sure that although physically alone, the child will feel and act under the protective eye of a caring and responsible parent. Every child deserves that. It's a critical part of what being a child is all about.

James Garbarino, Ph.D.

INTRODUCTION

Alone After School is a book that has been written out of a need both professional and personal. As the authors, we are not only experts in the field of latchkey children, but working parents whose own children require self-care.

Thus we bring both theory and practice to the page! Theory in our professional roles: Helen Swan (M.S.W., L.S.C.S.W.) is a nationally recognized expert on children in self-care. As a counselor and educator, she specializes in developing programs that deal with family issues. Victoria Houston is a writer whose award-winning articles on family issues have been nationally syndicated.

Practice in our daily lives: As mothers of children in self-care, we experience the problems and frustrations of planning good self-care — how to deal with lengthy daily commutes or long-distance travel, fluctuating work schedules, and the challenges of both urban and suburban living. We, like many working parents who are married or single, try to do this while making sure our children feel safe, emotionally secure, and have all the opportunities kids should have!

The Child in Self-Care

The last ten years have seen a rapid increase in the number of children staying home alone and caring for themselves. This self-care usually occurs during the daytime hours while parents are at work or involved in other activities. Most of these children are between the ages of eight and fifteen, they have two working parents or a single parent, and they are most often alone between the time that school lets out and parents return home.

While it is a known fact that the numbers of children in self-care, latchkey children, are steadily increasing, it is less known that these are children from families at *all* socioeconomic levels. Indeed, recent news stories point out that the higher the education level of the parents, the greater the likelihood of their having a latchkey child!

Experts Disagree

As the number of children in self-care grows, so do the disagreements among national experts on the effects of self-care. Some feel it is harmful, increasing a child's fears and the danger of physical harm while limiting opportunities to see and enjoy friends during a time of rapid emotional development. Others argue that this is not the case, that self-care encourages a child to assume the kind of responsibility that can lead to a strong and positive sense of self. They also stress the role the child can play as a significant contributor to the needs of the family.

This book does not presuppose whether self-care is "good or bad." Rather, the premise is that the *effect* of self-care is the result of many factors, and will be different for each family and child. Our intent is to inform parents and children of these factors so they may first tailor a family self-care plan to their own needs; and, second, be able to evaluate how this plan is working for their family. If, following this evaluation, a family chooses self-care, specific recommendations are included for self-care plans that will safeguard a child emotionally and physically.

The Self-Care Decision

Many parents tell us the decision to use self-care is very difficult. They have no way to judge if their child is really ready to be alone and they are not sure how to prepare the child for this experience. Often, it's difficult to judge whether the self-care plan a family chooses is adequate.

This book is intended to help parents with this decision by emphasizing the importance of choosing self-care *if it will serve the best interests of your child.*

Premature Self-Care

Premature placement in self-care can be physically and emotionally damaging for a young child because it "hurries" the child through childhood. Many experts feel that speeding up this transition from childhood to adolescence, which self-care can do, may create excess stress and ultimately affect the development of a child. Again, we encourage you to carefully evaluate your child's readiness through the use of this practical family guide.

Attitudes Toward the Latchkey Child

Community attitudes toward the latchkey child, a term commonly used to describe a child in self-care, can be negative and imply parental neglect or lack of control. If a family is sensitive to this, the guilt can have a negative effect on everyone, including the child. Remember that self-care can be a positive experience. Structure your plan well, evaluate it regularly, and feel confident that your family is working together in a direction that will benefit everyone.

How to Use This Book: Five Easy Steps

Alone After School is an easy-to-use workbook developed to encourage parents and children to discuss and make self-care decisions *together*. The exercises are designed to teach self-care skills as well as provide a good parent-child dialogue on self-care experiences, problems, and joys.

The sections on Emotional Health and Physical Safety highlight the information and skills necessary for *all* self-care plans. The sections on the care of brothers and sisters, teenagers, and summer self-care address more specialized needs of some families.

Step One: We recommend that parents read Chapters One through Four in order to understand the needs, responsibilities, and problems of families who choose self-care. In addition, parents will want to familiarize themselves with those chapters, such as "Summer Care," that also relate to the family's self-care situation. Finally, parents will want to glance at Chapters Five through Ten, which cover physical safety, in order to understand what will be expected of the child in self-care.

Step Two: Answering the question "Is My Child Ready?" in Chapter Fourteen is the next step if you continue to feel that self-care will work for your family. Here you find the issues presented in a way that will help you discuss self-care with all family members to ensure a clear understanding of everyone's needs.

Step Three: Chapter Fifteen, "How to Design Your Self-Care Plan," provides you with samples of rules and agreements that work well for many families.

Step Four: Once the decision to plan self-care has been made, it is time for the child who will be in self-care to read and complete Chapters Five through Ten. Parents should participate in and double-check all the activities presented in these chapters. (Note that parents have exercises, too, in Chapters One through Four on emotional health.)

Step Five: We ask you to pay special attention to Chapter Sixteen, "For Kids Only," and encourage your child to read it. Here, you and your child will find the candid remarks of children in self-care — their fears and their satisfactions. "For Kids Only" reinforces your child's need and right to be included in all self-care decisions.

This book should prove valuable as a reference book for as long as you and your family participate in self-care. As your child enters the teen years, or when summer rolls around, consult *Alone After School* for those recommendations that can help you through the rough spots.

Always remember that self-care does involve some risk for children. Kids are kids, after all, and in caring for themselves they are sure to make mistakes. Our primary goal in this book is to minimize the danger and to safeguard the health and happiness of your children — and ours!

CONTENTS

Chapter 10

GETTING INTO COOKING • 97

Chapter 11

BROTHERS AND SISTERS IN SELF-CARE • 123

Chapter 12

THE YOUNG TEEN • 136

Chapter 16
FOR KIDS ONLY • 181

1
PIONEERS OR GUILTY PARENTS?

The rise in the number of children in self-care is a direct reflection of the increase in the number of families with both parents working. This is a new dynamic in American family life; a dynamic that makes working parents today pioneers in establishing patterns of family living that are very different from their parents' and grandparents'.

Quite simply, parents today are raising their children differently. They are pioneers in a terrain fraught with anxiety and guilt. At the same time, however, they are pioneers in establishing new kinds of satisfaction, self-sufficiency, achievement, and family cooperation that can be enthusiastically shared by all family members. If the guilt and anxiety can be addressed and managed, what will remain is an exciting, challenging experience unique in family living today.

A PARENT'S GUILT

When parents leave children in self-care, they worry about the *child's* reaction to being alone. They seldom realize the stress this places on the parent as well. For this reason, self-care must be considered from two points of view — the parent's as well as the child's.

"Even though I can't afford to hire anyone to watch Teddy, I worry," said one working mother. "Every day at 3:15 I can feel myself tense up. Will he catch the bus? Did he get home okay? Is he safe? I worry every afternoon!"

Like many working parents, she bears the burden of a philosophy that has prevailed in America since the 1800s — a philosophy that states that the mother should be home with the child as the primary nurturer, wholly responsible for the child's physical and emotional growth and well-being. The father, on the other hand, is recognized as the breadwinner. Yet, in today's society, such families are in the minority. Most children live in families in which a mother is working or frequently away from the home.

As a result, many parents who choose self-care for their children feel an overwhelming sense of guilt — a guilt grounded in the negative feeling that they are not raising their children the way that they were raised. They also have few or no standards by which to judge whether or not they are raising their children successfully. Yet, early results are indicating that many children of working parents can do well, both emotionally and physically.

How to Handle Your Guilt

First, acknowledge that you can create a positive home environment for your children even though you work. Raising your children differently from the way you were raised can be a challenge — not a negative situation. Learn to recognize when you feel guilty because your parents "did it" differently, and when you feel guilty for other reasons.

Second, work to develop a good self-care plan — one that you feel covers all your family's needs. Then, knowing you have a comprehensive self-care plan, you will be able to communicate a feeling of security and well-being to your child. On the other hand, if your guilt makes you feel something is intrinsically wrong with self-care, your child will be aware of this even if he or she is doing well. Such feelings can sabotage the best efforts. You can avoid this by realistically assessing how strong your self-care plan is — just what this book is intended to do.

With a good self-care plan in place, monitor your own feelings as the family adjusts to the new schedules and agreements. As you watch your child take on each new responsibility — and do well — your feelings of guilt should begin to dissipate.

However, if these feelings persist after the initial settling-in period, your guilt may be a warning that something is indeed wrong. A feeling of guilt that persists or recurs may be a signal that it's time to strengthen your family's self-care plan or consider other alternatives.

You can reduce your feelings of guilt and defuse potential problems by taking a realistic look at the causes for your feelings. The following questions can help you do this. They will help you determine how you feel about leaving your child in self-care. There are no right and wrong answers; negative responses can be your most valuable tool for developing a sound self-care plan that will work for both you and your child.

When My Child Is Home Alone:

I worry about . . .

I would feel better if . . .

I am sometimes afraid that . . .

Do I worry about my child home alone?

1. Almost never   2. Sometimes   3. Most of the time   4. Always

Do I feel guilty about leaving my child home alone?

1. Almost never   2. Sometimes   3. Most of the time   4. Always

Do I feel good about how I fulfill my role as a parent?

How do my children really feel about my working?

List the kind of "quality time" you spend with your child:

Now examine each of your answers. Can you pinpoint particular problems that are causing you worry over your family's self-care situation? How frequently do you have these feelings?

Once you have identified your concerns and feelings, review Chapter Fourteen, "Is My Child Ready?" This will help you evaluate your child's self-care situation. Now go back and review your own concerns. How realistic are they? Are there ways you can help your child learn to manage in self-care that will help to decrease your own guilt?

Excessive Guilt

Remember, excessive guilt on the part of the parent can affect a child's performance in self-care. You want to be sure to evaluate your own feelings on a regular basis, just as you continue to observe your child's needs and feelings.

Children sometimes tell us that they like self-care, but that their moms and dads worry a lot. They wonder if their parents think they are unable to manage in self-care. "I feel okay most of the time," said one eleven-year-old boy, "but my mom and dad worry a lot. It makes me nervous — I wonder if they trust me."

Other children attempt to use a parent's anxiety as a way to place blame for their own misbehavior: "If you were home, this wouldn't happen."

In fact, acknowledging and working with your guilt can make it possible for you and your family to avoid these situations.

2
EMOTIONAL HEALTH

This chapter looks at the child in self-care with an emphasis on those skills parents and children can use to make the self-care experience emotionally satisfying for all family members.

Like most parents who choose self-care, you will probably experience great concern for your child's physical safety, and worry about break-ins, fires, or serious fights with brothers and sisters. Equally important, however, is how your child adjusts emotionally to being home alone.

You can begin to establish a good emotional environment by asking yourself the following questions:

1. Does my child feel good about being home alone in self-care? Does he or she express feelings of fear, loneliness, or boredom?

2. Does my child learn new skills easily and take pride in his or her accomplishments?

3. Do all our family members feel confident about our plans for self-care?

4. Does the self-care situation increase tensions for my child and our family?

As for asking yourself whether self-care will be emotionally harmful or helpful for your child, there are no easy answers.

Adults who have been in self-care report different reactions. Some feel that self-care helped them to be more responsible and was a way to contribute to the family; others feel that being home alone increased their feelings of rejection by parents and led to poor relationships with their brothers and sisters.

We do know, however, that children who are not ready to care for themselves often do not do well in self-care. We also know that a positive parent-child relationship is the cornerstone of a self-care situation in which children feel good about themselves and their family.

COMMUNICATION — THE KEY TO SELF-CARE

How do you know if self-care is helpful to the emotional well-being of your child? Such answers can be found only by keeping in close touch with your child—through communication and observation. The following will highlight ways to improve communication between parent and child; to deal with specific feelings of fear, loneliness, and boredom; and to structure self-care so that it increases a child's good feelings about self and family.

Communication between you and your child is the key to successful self-care. Yet, even the most well-meaning working parents often have difficulty finding time to discuss with children problems that arise in self-care. Such discussions are critical; these conversations are your way of assessing how your child is doing.

Begin talking with your child about self-care when you first consider it as a possibility. Familiarize yourself with the issues covered in this book. Note that Chapter Fourteen, "Is My Child Ready?" offers suggestions on how to determine if your child is ready for self-care.

We hope you will recognize that self-care is a joint responsibility between parents and children, that both share responsibilities to make self-care workable. You can foster this attitude by always including your child in the development of your family's self-care plan; by asking your child for his or her ideas and feelings.

HOW CAN I GET MY CHILD TO TALK ABOUT SELF-CARE?

1. Pick a time when you can really talk.
2. Listen to what the child has to say.

3. Be willing to accept your child's ideas; don't make fun of unworkable suggestions.
4. Praise your child for his or her participation.

Planning Talk Time

Talk doesn't just happen — you have to plan for it. We recommend that you plan a family meeting to discuss the agreements that will structure your self-care plan. The parent-child contract in Chapter Fifteen, "How to Design Your Self-Care Plan," will be helpful in setting the agenda for these meetings. Once the agreements are made, they must be reviewed regularly. The following suggestions have been helpful for most families.

Communication Roadblocks

In working with children in self-care, we've found that many are reluctant to share feelings and problems with parents. Here are some signals to watch for and some hints for turning potential problem areas into avenues of good communication.

The "I've Got to Be Happy" Syndrome

Most children we talk with in self-care report that they are happy, and indeed many appear to be. However, children will sometimes say they are happy because they know that their parents want them to be. When asking children who are obviously unhappy in family situations to draw a picture of how they really feel, children will often draw a frown, erase it, and draw a happy face. Sometimes children feel that they will disappoint their parents if they are not happy.

Other times, children hide their feelings about self-care because they know there are no other choices for their parents. "If I tell my mom that I don't like being home alone, it will only make her feel bad," reported one child we talked with. "I know she can't afford to stay home with me."

Adults who have experienced self-care report always wishing that their parents, especially their mother, had been home more. Children in self-care say the same thing. However, wishing a parent were home more does not mean that self-care is causing unhappiness. Even children whose mothers are home full-time will say they wish their parents were home more!

Solution: Encourage your child to be honest about self-care. Let each child know that you will not be upset if he or she does not like staying home alone. Even if you cannot change the self-care arrangements, just listening will often make your child feel better. It could lead to small but significant changes in the self-care plan.

"We Won't Talk" Responses

Many times in self-care situations, children are unwilling to share problems with their parents. Frequently, they're fearful that they will get in trouble. Other times, they feel that they are tattling on a brother or sister. One parent reported coming home one evening and finding the lamp broken in the living room. She asked her two children what happened. Her youngest daughter said, "Mom, we would rather not talk about it." It is difficult to expect children in such a situation to talk freely.

Solutions: Encourage and praise your child for sharing any problems in self-care. Emphasize that this is not tattling. Always respond to the sharing of problems in a supportive way. Look to solve the problem, not to punish.

Do not expect your children to share the news that they have broken the rules. In the case of a broken lamp, ask what happened. If your children do not respond, ask both to clean up the mess and decide later if any further action is necessary.

"It's Not What I Say, But What I Do."

How a child feels is only one measure of whether self-care is the appropriate day-care choice. For many of the children we talked with, it was apparent that they enjoyed the situation. However, in reviewing how they cared for themselves or their brothers and sisters, there were often areas of serious concern.

While a child may enjoy autonomy in being home alone, this autonomy could include not following rules, engaging in behavior that the parents would not approve of, and harassing younger brothers and sisters. Thus, it is important that parents not only ask about a child's feelings, but also continue to evaluate how a child manages the freedoms of self-care.

"An Ounce of Prevention"

Parents can often prevent problems with their child in self-care situations by carefully planning before placing their child in self-care.

Evaluate each child's needs for social contacts and activities. Some children are less social than others; having a friend visit once or twice a week may be sufficient. Other children require a great deal of social contact and have a short attention span. These children can be easily bored or lonely when home alone.

Most children, as they approach adolescence, require more contact with peers. To prevent problems, try to develop plans that meet the needs—individual and age appropriate—for each child. Review Chapter Fourteen, "Is My Child Ready?"

3

FAMILIAR FEELINGS: FEAR, LONELINESS, AND BOREDOM

Children in self-care often report feelings of fear, loneliness, and boredom. Experts differ in their opinions on whether children in self-care experience these feelings more frequently than children who are supervised. One study clearly shows that self-care children in a rural area adjust as well socially and have no more fears than supervised children. The key factor appears to be the safety of the neighborhood. In a safe neighborhood, children have more freedom and, in turn, adjust better.

FEAR

All children experience fear. Fear is a natural response to a situation with which one feels unable to cope. Common fears that children in self-care report are:

1. Physical injury: break-ins, fights with brothers and sisters, assaults by strangers

2. Accidents: fires, physical injury, property damage
3. Injury to parents: late coming home, not calling on time

Any unpredictable event can cause a child to be fearful when home alone. One girl shared her reaction to a common fear experienced by children home alone: the doorbell ringing. "I hid behind the chair, then crawled on my stomach to the back door. After ten minutes, I ran to the neighbors. I felt so dumb when I found out it was a man delivering pizza and he came to the wrong house."

Girls often report more fears than boys when home alone; younger children usually experience and report more imaginary fears such as someone in the house or people following them home. Most children express more fear when they are home alone at night than during the day.

What to Do to Quiet a Child's Fear

A parent can make many responses that will help a child handle fear. First, encourage your child to talk about fears. This can be done in the following ways:

1. Be a role model. When you yourself are concerned or worried, demonstrate to your child an appropriate way to discuss fear.

   "John, I was really worried when you were late coming home from work. I thought there might have been an accident."

   At the same time, a parent should not be too open; a parent can talk a child into being fearful if too much is made of a situation.

2. Ask your child specific questions about feelings when home alone:

   "Do you ever feel afraid when you are home alone? What do you do?"

   "Do you ever feel scared when the doorbell rings and you are home alone? What do you do?"

   "Do you check to see if the house is safe when you first come home? What do you do?"

3. Respect a child's fear. Do not try to judge whether he or she is wrong. Fear is a very potent feeling. Never make fun of your child when he or she talks about fear.

4. Praise your child when he or she discusses fears. "I understand why you were afraid. Thanks for telling me. Now I can help."

5. Have your child complete the exercises in "Scary Noises," in Chapter Six.

Note: A child's response on how he or she handles each situation will help you evaluate how intense the fears are. For example, a child who hides in a closet is more fearful than a child who does not answer the door and simply remains quiet.

Prepare your child so that he or she feels safe when home alone. Consider your answers to the following questions:

1. Do I tell my child when I will be home?
2. Do I always arrive home on time?
3. Do I leave a phone number where I can be reached?
4. Have I instructed my child to handle emergencies? Fires? Strangers? Injuries?

As mentioned earlier, fear is a response a child feels when he or she feels unable to cope. Thus, helping a child think of possible responses when afraid will often help dispel fears:

1. Have the child decide if there is an immediate danger. For example, is someone looking in the window, or did the child hear a noise in the house that he or she has heard before? Although fear is not rational, try and encourage the child to think through whether there is an immediate danger.

2. Have the child list solutions. In situations where a child feels there is an immediate danger, decide together if the child should call a parent, a neighbor, or the police. It may be necessary to leave the house.

Make a list of possible responses for a child to use when something less serious happens, such as hearing a strange noise in the house. Responses that children frequently find comforting include turning up the television or radio, hiding, calling a friend, playing a game, reading, or inspecting the house.

3. If the fear continues, have your child call you or another adult. If your child calls, repeat steps 1 and 2 by phone.

4. We have written sections on physical safety specifically to help children feel safe and learn how to cope with many problems. Encourage your child to complete all the exercises in Chapters Five through Ten.

LONELINESS

Feelings of loneliness differ greatly among children in self-care. Some seem to enjoy being home alone while others complain frequently of being lonely. Most children report that they would like to have more after-school activities.

"It's o.k. being home alone," said one ten-year-old girl. "But I wish that I could do more things after school. The only time I see my friends is at Girl Scouts every two weeks."

More often, however, children in self-care complain about not seeing friends. These complaints increase among teenagers for whom peer contact is extremely important. "The worst thing about being home alone is that my parents won't let me have any friends over," said one twelve-year-old boy. "It's not fair, why should I be punished because my parents work?"

How to Help Your Child Deal with Loneliness

You can help your child with feelings of loneliness by working together to find ways to reduce these feelings. Begin by making a list of the different responses he or she might have when feeling lonely. The following might be included.

1. Invite a friend home (with permission!)
2. Visit a friend or neighbor.
3. Talk on the phone.
4. Play with a pet.
5. Meet a friend at the library or shopping center.

Should Friends Visit Children Who Are Home Alone?

Many parents are reluctant to allow their child to visit or have friends in the home to play when an adult is not there to supervise.

Concern over accidents, misbehavior, and financial liability is something that each parent must consider. Yet, contact with friends is an important part of growing up.

Common rules that parents often have for children and their friends include the following.

1. Your friends are or are not allowed in our house when we are not home.
2. Your friends are or are not allowed to play in our yard.
3. With permission from us, you may visit friends; be sure to tell us where you will be and when you will return.

Review with your child the following safety concerns in making a decision about having friends visit.

	Yes	No
Is our neighborhood safe?	___	___
Do your friend's parents approve of their child being in our home unsupervised?	___	___
Does your friend seem mature enough to be home alone with you? (Evaluate past behavior.)	___	___
Are you mature enough to be home alone with a friend? (Evaluate past behavior.)	___	___
Which of our friends or neighbors are the best for you to visit?		

If the answer to any of these questions is "no," you may need to place some limitations on self-care visiting privileges for your child. If you and your child agree that having friends in your home or visiting their homes is acceptable, these visits should be carefully structured. See Chapter Fifteen, "How to Design Your Self-Care Plan," for help in setting up these agreements.

BOREDOM

Some children complain that being in self-care is boring. "It's boring. There isn't anything to do," they say. All children experience being bored — particularly in adolescence. When children in self-care report these feelings, a parent can help the child find constructive ways to use time.

How to Help Your Child Avoid Boredom

Most children can take some action to avoid constant feelings of boredom. Remind your child that being bored is a choice, that you can choose not to be bored. Work with your child to develop a list of things to do to avoid boredom:

Play a game.	Start a hobby.
Read a book.	Do homework.
Watch TV.	Listen to music.
Call a friend.	Cook a meal or treat.
Do a chore.	Play with a pet.

Parents can support their child's efforts to stay busy by taking their child to the library regularly, collecting needed supplies for projects, encouraging hobbies, and by praising a child when free time has been used constructively.

The Parent Surprise

You can also keep looking for new ideas — suprises you can save for the day when everything seems boring. "Look in my bottom drawer, I have a new game for you, a new notebook, or a new book."

These surprises can become an interesting challenge for both you and your child. Feel free to set limits; for example, no more than two surprises a month.

EXCESSIVE FEAR, LONELINESS, AND BOREDOM

While parents and children work on feelings of fear, loneliness, and boredom, parents need to be able to recognize when things are not working well. Depression, excessive fear, or other strong feelings can be harmful to the emotional health of your child.

What specific behavior can a parent watch for that might indicate that a child is having a problem with self-care? Any of the following are clues that a child home alone may be overly fearful, bored, lonely, or unhappy.

1. Recurring nightmares in which the child is helpless or powerless in the dream. Children often report nightmares after any major life change. If the dreams continue for a period of time, it is usually an indication that a child is having problems coping with some part of his or her life.
2. Depressive behavior such as loss of appetite, lack of interest in activities, frequent crying spells, irritability, or frequent loss of temper.
3. Frequent complaints of feeling lonely, bored, or fearful.

If your child displays any of these characteristics, parents and child should work to change the self-care situation to better meet the needs of the child. Consider one or more of the following suggestions with your child.

1. Reduce the number of hours that your child is home alone.
2. Review and try earlier solutions recommended for fear, loneliness, and boredom.
3. Plan to have your child stay with a neighbor or friend part of the time.
4. Listen to your child's feelings; perhaps check in more often each day.
5. Make other arrangements for your child.
6. Seek professional help.

PETS

Pets can be of special value in self-care. "I always get my two dogs from the back yard before I go in the house," said one ten-year-old girl. "Just having the dogs with me makes me feel safe."

"When I have nothing to do," one eleven-year-old boy said, "I take my dogs for a walk. They really like it and I have a good time, too."

Another nine-year-old girl said, "I always watch television with my cat. It is nice having her with me even though she doesn't really watch TV."

TELEVISION

The television set is one of the most constant companions of children who are home alone. Research shows that children in self-care watch TV an average of four to five hours a day. Adolescents, ages ten to fifteen years old, watch TV an average of twenty-three hours a week. From all reports, watching television is the favorite activity of children home alone after school.

While television, at its best, may be entertaining, the benefits that children receive from constant daily watching are questionable. Children report that after-school TV usually consists of sitcoms or soap operas; little of value is offered that provides a healthy influence in regard to career decisions, personal relationships, or sexuality.

What can a parent do to influence a child's choice of programs in after-school hours? How can a child be encouraged to select TV programs that incorporate the values of the family? The following suggestions have been used by other parents to encourage children to "turn off the television."

1. Make up a television schedule each week. Ask all your children in self-care to participate. The schedule will alert you to what they are watching as well as help brothers and sisters settle disputes. One mother reported that the schedule was taped next to the television set and resolved many family arguments.

2. Be a role model. Turn off the television set when you see that a program is poor or depicts values that are not helpful for your children.

3. Encourage your child to participate in other activities including music lessons, sports, and hobbies that will result in "turning off the tube."

4. Remember, you cannot enforce rules about what children watch on TV when you are not at home.

4

FEELING GOOD IN SELF-CARE

A positive self-care situation is one in which children can assume home responsibilities and feel good about their accomplishments. Many children we have talked with report those exact feelings. When asked how they feel, they say "responsible." When asked what they do well when home alone, these remarks are often made: "I do chores," "I know how to take care of my brothers and sisters," "I can cook," and "I'm good at watching myself."

What can a parent do to make self-care a positive experience in which the child learns responsibility and feels good in self-care? Our review of many self-care situations, shows that parents who take the time to teach their children responsibilities and praise their actions appear to have the most successful self-care plans.

PRAISE

Just as the expectations that parents have for children in self-care situations differ, so do the responsibilities. For example, sample surveys reflect that from fifty percent to ninety percent of parents assign chores to children. In other homes, the expectation of a parent is simply "to take good care of yourself." While children generally report that they dislike doing chores, when asked what they do well in self-care, they list *with pride* the chores that they complete!

Even if you do not assign chores for your child, you can use praise to help your child feel happy and safe in self-care. As you spend time each evening talking with your child about how the day has gone, always include one positive comment about your child's behavior. You might make comments like the following.

"You certainly followed the rules well today."

"I'm really pleased at how well you did taking care of yourself."

"You did your homework already? Boy, you are really organized!"

"You are so responsible! I'm proud."

It is even more important to make a positive comment to a child when things have not gone well. Blaming a child for what went wrong may correct a problem but it will not help a child feel good about self-care. For example, you might say: "I'm comfortable that you will know how to handle the problem now," rather than: "You know better than that. Don't ever do that again."

Reward Systems

Many of the self-care families we've talked with have designed formal check systems that work well to reward responsible behavior. In most situations, children are rewarded for following the rules or completing chores. The most common rewards are special outings on the weekends such as movies, skating, extra allowance, or shopping trips. Special privileges each night might be TV or treats.

The mother of a nine-year-old boy designed the following reward system for following the rules.

Rules	M	T	W	Th	F
Call me when you come home.	x	x	x	x	x
Stay in the house.	x		x	x	x
Do not answer the phone or door.	x	x	x	x	x
Hang up your coat.	x		x	x	
Clean up after you eat.	x		x		x

The child receives ten cents for each x, totaling two dollars a week. Every six months the mother and child change some of the rules so that the child is able to learn new responsibilities. The mother also feels that the chart is an easy way to review each day.

The following plan was designed by the parents of fifteen- and twelve-year-old daughters.

Chores and Rules	M	T	W	Th	F
Call me before leaving the house.	x		x	x	x
No friends in the house.	x	x	x	x	x
Chores					
Clean the kitchen (M)	x				
Vacuum the living room (T)		x			
Clean your room (W)			x		
Enjoy a day off! (Th)				x	
Pick up the living room (F)					x

The following suggestions were offered by the parents who designed this system.

1. Walk through each chore when assigning it so that the child understands what is required and how to complete the chore.

2. Check each night to make sure the chore is completed as agreed upon.

3. Change chores frequently. Children often complain about doing the same chore each day. This family lists all chores to be done. From that list, each child picks two and the parents assign two so that both children have an equal number of responsibilities.

4. Separate brothers and sisters. Each child should have a separate chart, and chores might be assigned in different rooms to limit conflict.

AGE-APPROPRIATE RESPONSIBILITY

For a child to feel successful in self-care, responsibilities and house rules should be age-appropriate. One major reason some children do poorly in self-care is that they are not ready to assume the responsibilities of taking care of themselves or others. Selecting house rules and responsibilities that a child can successfully perform is critical to a positive sense of self-esteem in self-care.

For example, rules for a nine-year-old child in self-care might include:

No friends are allowed in the house to play.

Do not answer the phone.

Do not answer the door.

Parents, when questioned why they have chosen these rules, say they feel that their child is still young enough to be tricked into saying a parent is not home. This is why they make self-care rules for younger children that require very simple responses. Such rules, while socially more confining, can be successfully handled by a younger child.

On the other hand, parents report the following rules for adolescents.

- You are allowed to have friends over after calling for permission each time.
- You must leave a note before leaving the house to meet friends.
- Do not let strangers into the home. Tell them your parents cannot come to the door.
- Do not let strangers into the home. Tell them your parents cannot come to the door.

Again, parents report that these rules reflect their child's maturity and ability to respond. Most adolescents, when not responsible for younger children, need and should have more social freedom.

Selecting home responsibilities that a child can successfully perform requires the same principles as having house rules. Decisions by parents are often based upon the interest, motor skills, and time required for each task. For example, a nine-year-old child home alone for two hours might be required to do one of the chores listed below:

Take out the trash.

Put away the dishes.

Dust or sweep.

Clean your bedroom.

Make cold treats or sandwiches.

A child age eleven or older is capable of doing most home chores once he or she has received instructions. Children usually feel positive about the experience if the following points are considered:

1. The chores should not require a great deal of time. Children like and need time to relax and pursue other interests.

2. The child should have some input as to which chores are required.

3. The child should be able to do the chore. Making children responsible for putting away dishes they might break, cleaning that can't be managed with the vacuum cleaner, or cooking with an unfamiliar stove will only lead to conflict between parent and child.

How do you know when your child is able to perform a chore or follow a rule? The only way is to teach your child the task and test to see if he or she is capable of the responsibility. Remember, if your child is not ready to follow rules or complete chores, punishment is not the solution. These are signals that your child is not ready for the task or is not ready to be home alone in self-care.

TIME WITH PARENTS

Just as feeling good about oneself is important in a self-care situation, so is feeling good about one's parents. One major element that determines whether a child does well in self-care is the parent-child relationship. When parents and their child have a good, strong relationship before self-care, the self-care experience reflects this. Such a relationship must be nurtured throughout the entire self-care experience.

Time is a priceless commodity for working parents; it is always too short to do all that must be done. We know that time with our children is necessary for their social, emotional, and intellectual development. Current studies indicate that many children learn less today because they have less contact with significant adults than in past generations.

Teenagers, according to current studies, also say that what they want most from their parents is to talk to them and have them listen. Not only are parents absent more, but grandparents, neighbors, and teachers are also less available to spend time with children. Thus, children in today's world look more to their parents for attention.

How much time does a child need with parents? The common response is "as much or more than you can give." Actually, such a question is difficult to answer. Each child has different needs for attention and direction from a parent. Some require little, while others seem to need constant structure and attention. We know that all children need a regular time each day when parent and child can be together.

Children in self-care often want a great deal of attention and direction, especially when they first begin caring for themselves. Not only is the child learning new skills, but he or she may still feel ambivalent about being home alone.

If a parent has not worked before, a child may resent changes in family life. In some cases, children may feel rejected when a parent is first employed. Clear explanations of why a parent is working can often help prevent these negative feelings.

Many self-care situations are the result of other family crises such as a divorce. In these cases, a child may also need to relocate, attend a new school, and have his or her mother begin work. This child will require more understanding and attention, often at a time when neither parent is well-equipped to meet these needs.

One eleven-year-old girl we talked with described such a situation as she said, crying, "I am so unhappy. I miss both my mom and dad. My dad has moved away and my mom has a new job and doesn't have much time." After talking together, mother and daughter decided how more time could be spent together.

Quality Time

In the last few years there has been a great deal of emphasis on "quality time" with children. Quality time refers to "time more enriching than normal experiences — time that pays close attention to the needs of the child." The concept of quality time has sometimes been interpreted to mean that parents can spend less time with their children as long as it is quality time.

Whether such an idea is true or not is still disputed. We do know, however, that children need both time and quality. There are no shortcuts, particularly for children who are in self-care on a regular basis.

Finding Time

How can parents find more time for their children? The first step is determining how your time is now spent. To assess your family schedule, complete the following questionnaire by listing the average number of hours spent each week in the following activities.

Activity	Hours per day				
	M	T	W	Th	F
Work hours					
Household chores					
Time for self					
Time for spouse alone					
Time for children					

Add the numbers of hours for each category. A normal week would consist of 112 hours (16 hours × 7 days). By dividing your total by 112 hours, you can find the percentage of time you spent each week in each category.

After evaluating the time spent with your children, consider the following suggestions for increasing the time available for your children.

1. Household Chores. This category is often the one that most easily can be changed. Can some of the chores be managed by domestic help? Can the children assume some of the responsibilities? Can some of the chores be done with your children? Trips to the store? Dinner dishes? Cleaning the living room? Often, chores can be done while spending time with the children.

2. Adult Time. Are there other adults who can spend time with your child? A neighbor? A grandparent? A friend? Can you and the other parent divide some of the time and responsibilities of being with your child?

3. Scheduled Time. Plan time each day to talk with your child. At mealtime? Early evening? Bedtime? Use this time to find out how the day went and to have fun.

4. Planned Activities. Have fun with your child. Choose activities that both of you enjoy — homework, reading a story, or watching TV. Allow for activities that take more time such as doing a puzzle, or taking a walk.

Take time now to enjoy your child. It is the best gift you can give!

5

PHYSICAL SAFETY

This is a very important chapter for every one of you who will be spending some time home alone. Your safety is the most serious concern your parents have as they ask you to take care of yourself.

In another part of this book we talk about your feelings and how well you are able to manage your feelings when you're alone. Now we are most concerned with keeping you safe. That is why you have this book in your hands at this moment!

Why are the grown-ups around you so concerned? If some emergency happens, or if you get sick, they won't be there to help — at least, not right away. They want to be sure that you know just what to do.

We know this is very important because our research — that is all the questions that we've asked people all over the country — shows that eight percent of all children left to care for themselves will face serious emergencies. What does that mean? Simply, this: If you have 100 kids in your school who go home to a house where they will be alone for awhile after school, 8 of those kids will have something serious happen like a fire or a broken bone or a stranger who tries to hurt them.

We want to be sure that if you are one of those children, *you will know exactly what to do*. We want to be sure that if one of those children is a friend of yours, *you will be able to help*. We want you to feel so sure of how you will handle yourself in an emergency that you will feel comfortable being alone, and when problems come up — even if you get scared — you always know what to do to help yourself.

Children are able to handle emergencies at a very young age, as long as someone has shown them what to do. One seven-year-old girl was out playing by herself one day when she saw a very old lady fall down on the sidewalk by her house. The girl ran to her mother and told her to call an ambulance to help the lady. She felt very frightened when she saw the lady fall, but she also felt strong when she saw the ambulance come to help her. That seven-year-old was able to do what grown-ups do. That's exactly what we are going to teach each of you.

We feel that just *reading* how to be safe isn't enough, so we are writing this with lots of practice exercises. Then, your mom or dad or other relative should do some of these exercises with you. That will help them feel better about your ability to care for yourself at the same time that you are learning what to do. You may want to do some of these exercises with a friend. They can be fun even if we're talking about something very serious. There are some exercises that a teacher may want to do with everyone in your class.

THE FOUR STEPS TO SAFETY

We want you to think about each emergency that we are going to look at as if there were four steps to learning how to handle the crisis:

- **Step 1: What to Do:** the right action to take in an emergency.
- **Step 2: How It Can Happen:** a true story of how this happened to a young person alone.
- **Step 3: Let's Imagine:** finding some locations in your home and some reasons why this emergency or crisis *could* happen to you.
- **Step 4: Practice:** exercises that help you practice what you need to know in order to handle an emergency.

These four steps will be described for each major emergency. First, let's talk about your most important tool for good self-care — your telephone.

THE TELEPHONE — YOUR LIFELINE

You need the telephone for many reasons: for safety, for staying in touch with your parents so they know you are fine, and for keeping in touch with friends just to chat.

In fact, the telephone is so important to you that if you don't have one, please ask your mom or dad to consider the extra expense *just for your safety*. If you do have one, always be sure to have it fixed immediately if it should ever be broken.

Because the telephone is your lifeline in case of emergencies, you should practice using it for several different purposes.

Keeping in Touch with Parents

Let's begin with your mom and dad. All of you should decide together when you will call them or if they will be calling you.

- Are there times when it is difficult to reach your parents at work? _____
- Do you have to call their place of work and leave a special message in order to reach them? _____
- Should you call only once or more often? _____
- Is there a special signal you can use so that you know it is Mom or Dad calling? For example, have them let the phone ring three times, and hang up; then call back. _____
- Will you check in every day and call back to let them know if you are leaving the house? _____
- Is there a time that you can call Mom or Dad and chat for a few minutes about how the day went? _____ This is the kind of call that can make you feel comfortable and not so much alone.
- Many children feel better if they receive a call every day when they get home from school. Is there a good time for your parents to call you each day? _____

Chatting with Friends

What about friends? We know that many of you who are teenagers or just about to become teenagers really depend on the phone to keep in touch with friends. This is important and something that parents should know. Phone contact with friends can help children in self-care feel much less lonely. Decide how long phone calls can be. _____ Consider having a "call waiting" feature on your phone in case a parent is trying to reach you during one of your chats with friends. "Call waiting" allows you to talk with another caller and still hold your first call on the line.

Calling for Help

First, sit down with your parents and make a list of the emergency phone numbers you will need. Then tape that list right beside your phone. If you have more than one phone, it is wise to have a list by each, particularly if you have one in a distant place such as the basement.

Special Note: It is an excellent idea to carry a copy of the list with you; in your wallet or purse, or slipped into a little plastic case so you can stick it into your pocket. At the same time, always keep enough money with your phone list to make a call from a pay telephone. This prepares you for emergencies away from home.

My Emergency Phone Numbers

My Name _____

Home Address _____

_____

Home Phone Number _____

Mom's Name _____

Mom's Work Phone _____

Dad's Name _____

Dad's Work Phone _____
Directions to my home from different locations, so I can tell people how to find me:

Special Note: Can you call 911 for emergency aid in your community? If so, you can call 911 for all emergency needs. If you do not have 911, you need these numbers:

Police Department _____

Fire Department _____

Ambulance/Hospital _____

Doctor _____

Poison Center _____

These numbers are just as important:

Neighbor _____

Neighbor _____

Relative _____

Friend _____

Friend's Parent Who Might Help _____

As you decide on these phone numbers, you will also be deciding some other important matters. Work with your parents to answer these questions:

- Whom should you call first in an emergency — Mom or Dad?
- Whom should you call if you cannot reach a parent?
- What should you do if you miss your bus and are stranded somewhere?
- What should you do if you have a problem and can't seem to reach any of the right people? Is there a friend whose parents might be able to help? Someone else? A friend of your mom's or dad's? A teacher? Someone at your church?

- If you can't think of anyone to call, remember, you can always call the police and just say "I'm desperate." You may be embarrassed, but you'll be safe!
- Now, add those phone numbers to your list. Check your list regularly so it is always current. Because this list is so important to you, we will schedule a regular check on the "Family Calendar." (See page 179.)

USING THE TELEPHONE:
THE FOUR STEPS TO SAFETY

Step 1: What to Do

Here is how to place an emergency call for fire. Check your list, whether it's in your pocket or by the phone, and call the emergency service you need. When you hear someone answer, say quickly and clearly:

> I have an emergency. I have a fire in the kitchen and the address is _____. My name is John Mitchell.

The person on the emergency line will ask you a quick question or two to be sure they have the right address, and the right directions. They may ask you to stay on the phone if you are calling from a neighbor's phone. They may tell you to be sure to leave your home immediately.

Do it this way for every emergency, always saying exactly what is happening *first*.

Step 2: How It Can Happen

A fire can happen very easily. One morning, ten-year-old Karen's mother spilled some butter onto the burner of their electric stove. She was in a rush and said she would clean it up that evening. Karen forgot about that. When she got home from school, she decided to warm up some milk for hot cocoa. Suddenly she heard a popping sound and saw flames under the milk pan. When she grabbed the pan away, the flames shot up and ignited some grease on the hood above the stove. It looked to Karen as if the whole stove top was in flames!

She ran from the house and banged on their neighbor's door. When the door opened, she rushed right to the telephone and called the fire department. Her neighbor had been asked if Karen might call on her in an emergency, so she also had a list of emergency numbers posted.

It was less than five minutes from when the fire started, to the arrival of the fire trucks. By that time, the fire had burned itself out, although the kitchen was smoky and the hood of the stove had burned. The firemen told Karen that her family was lucky. If the stove had been under cabinets, it might have been a worse fire but Karen's quick call would have made it possible for the firemen to keep it from spreading.

Step 3: Let's Imagine

Now think of several reasons why you might have to make an emergency call from your home. You give one reason, and ask your parents to give another. Think about accidents, strangers, animals, funny noises. What else?

Together, write your list here:

Step 4: Practice

Now, with a parent watching and listening, run to a room where an emergency might occur. Pretend that this emergency is indeed happening and describe what you see. Go to the nearest phone, find the number you need, and make the call. Hold down the receiver so the call doesn't actually go through, but say everything you would if the emergency were real. Besides giving your address, be sure you also *give directions to your home.* Can your parent understand what you are saying? Are your directions clear?

Remember, you may feel a little silly practicing at first, but everyone involved in helping you during an emergency practices regularly. At school you call that practice a drill such as fire drill.

Your police or fire department might call their practice an emergency drill or "dry run."

One of the most important reasons for this practice is to become so familiar with the way you need to move and to talk, that you can do it without thinking when you are under stress during a real emergency.

Special Note: By now you may feel there are some phone numbers you would like to memorize. This is an excellent idea. Practice with a friend or a parent.

OBSCENE OR THREATENING CALLS: THE FOUR STEPS TO SAFETY

In Chapter 15, "How to Design Your Self-Care Plan," we ask you and your family to decide if you will answer the phone when home alone, or if you will answer only special calls that can be recognized by a prearranged signal.

We do this because some people try to use the telephone to frighten others. They do this by making obscene phone calls in which the caller talks about sex or threatening calls that are meant to scare you.

Both kinds of calls are very frightening, especially if you are home alone. Just remember that it happens to everyone, so don't ever hesitate to tell someone right away. Chances are you were called just because your telephone number is in a phone book or the caller made up a number and it happened to be yours.

Step 1: What to Do

Since the obscene or threatening phone caller wants a response from you, the best way to stop the calls is to *say nothing but hang up immediately*. Then, call your parent or the person you need to reach first in an emergency.

If the calls persist, call the police and the telephone company. Be sure to tell them that you are young and home by yourself when this happens. Check with your mom or dad to see if they want to call the police or telephone company themselves.

If the caller cannot get you to talk back or to stay on the telephone and listen, *he probably won't call more than once or twice.*

Also, if you have received a bad call and you answer the phone only to hear no one talk at first, hang up. That pause when no one says anything on the other end of the line may mean it is the bad caller again. If it isn't, the person will call you back and talk faster so you'll know that the call is okay.

Step 2: How It Can Happen

Lisa, age fourteen, had just gotten home from school one rainy day. Her family lived on the thirteenth floor of a tall building in Boston, and when she talked on the telephone, she could look through the window and see almost the whole city. The phone rang and she answered happily, noticing how cloudy and dark the city seemed. It took a moment before she realized what the man's voice was saying. First, he called her by name. Then, he used words she'd heard at school — some were bad and some she didn't recognize. She also didn't know exactly what he meant, but she didn't like the sound of his voice. She hung up without saying anything.

Lisa leaned back against the wall, shaking. She didn't know what to do. The phone rang again. She let it ring and ring. She didn't answer it. When the ringing stopped, she called her mother at work and told her what happened.

"Write down what he said," said Lisa's mother. "I'll keep it to tell the phone company in case he calls again. That way, if this person is calling other people, they'll be able to know if it is the same caller. Write it down and then try to forget it."

After they talked awhile and Lisa's mother pointed out that the man could not get into their building, she called a neighbor and arranged for Lisa to spend the rest of the afternoon in the neighbor's apartment. As it turned out, Lisa did not get any more calls. Weeks later, at school, the principal asked if anyone had received obscene phone calls. Then Lisa discovered that almost every girl student had been called. Someone had used the school directory! Eventually, the police and telephone company found the person.

Most of the time, obscene and threatening phone calls only happen once or twice — as long as you hang up right away!

Step 3: Let's Imagine

Talk this over with your family. Do you know anyone who has received frightening calls like this? What did they do? Do you understand what an obscene call is? Your parents should discuss with you the kinds of things you might hear in such a call. As you are old enough to be home by yourself, you are old enough to know what "bad words" are.

Step 4: Practice

Start by pretending you are doing something very pleasant such as reading a favorite book or working on a school project, when you receive a frightening phone call. Decide whom to call first.

Now, practice placing the call and telling the person what happened. Decide what to do next. If you are going to be going to a neighbor or friend's house, include them in this practice.

Finally, discuss how you will feel about answering the phone after such an experience. Will you want to change your phone rules for a while? Answer only calls that have prearranged signals so you know it is a parent or friend?

Special Note: Three other kinds of calls to practice are these:

1. Ask a parent to pretend to be a stranger calling with a good reason for you to give your address. What should you say? *Never* give that information to anyone who calls you on the phone. Just ask the caller to leave a phone number and say that someone will call back.

2. Ask a friend to pretend to be calling one of your parents. What should you say? *Never* say that your mom and dad are not at home. Simply say that they cannot come to the phone at the moment. Ask the caller for a number, then call your parent at work and tell him or her about the call.

3. Ask a friend to pretend to be calling a wrong number and ask you "what number is this?" *Never* give a caller your number. Instead, ask "what number are you calling?" You can tell them if they reached that number or not, but you should not tell them your own number.

PHONEFRIEND — A SPECIAL SERVICE FOR CHILDREN IN SELF-CARE

Many people have recognized that a child in self-care can get lonely or bored or frightened. One group, the American Association of University Women (AAUW), has done something about it. They have begun a telephone service just for children in self-care; they call it "PhoneFriend."

PhoneFriend is a number you can call just for someone to talk to. The person you reach will be happy to talk with you about your day or your problems. PhoneFriend is also a good way to get help if you need it. The trained volunteer you talk with can help you with everything from pet care to first aid or just give you a little reassurance.

To find out if there is a PhoneFriend in your area, your family can check the phone book. Also, PhoneFriend Central has set up a networking project to help people establish a PhoneFriend in their community. In order to receive information on how to do this, including training manuals and an audio training tape, your parents can call PhoneFriend Central at (814) 466-7524. Some areas do have PhoneFriend, but call it a different name; you can call the PhoneFriend Central number in order to find that out, too.

Special Note: A PhoneFriend can never take the place of a call from your mom or dad, nor can it provide the supervision a child needs if a parent is not at home.

If you do have a PhoneFriend in your community, place that number on your special phone list.

6
YOUR HOME

The big key to home safety is to *be prepared*. Each of the following sections will help you do that. We hope you will be able to work with your family on all of the projects we recommend.

HOME EMERGENCY KIT

To be prepared for all home emergencies, you will need a "home emergency kit." First, find a good-sized cardboard box that will hold everything, and a notebook large enough to draw in. Your box will keep everything in one convenient place — all family members will be happy to know this — and your notebook will explain how to use each item as well as how to follow different procedures when emergencies arise.

POWER PROBLEMS

The electricity in your home may go out in the event of a major storm, a fire in the neighborhood, or heavy use in the summertime. With your family, do the following:

1. Locate your fuse box or circuit breaker and learn how to change fuses or switch off the circuit breakers.
2. Practice doing exactly that and write the instructions in your notebook. Be sure to draw diagrams to remind yourself where things are, what direction to turn switches, etc.

3. Put spare parts in your home emergency kit. Write down the phone number of your electric company in case you want to check with them for any reason.

4. If you live in an apartment building, write down the names and phone numbers of people to call if you have problems with electricity. A maintenance person? A main office person?

The gas for your home heating units or appliances can also be cut off or may need to be cut off in an emergency. With your family do the following:

1. Determine if you have gas coming into your home and locate where and how it can be turned off.

2. Practice doing that and write the instructions with diagrams in your notebook. Ask about the possibility of floods and whether or not you have washing machines, dryers, or hot water heaters that would need to have the gas turned off.

3. Are there phone numbers that are needed such as the local gas company? A local service person?

4. Note that if you ever smell gas around your home — inside or outside — you should call the gas company immediately. If you cannot reach them, call the fire department.

5. If you live in an apartment, are there special instructions for gas emergencies?

WATER PROBLEMS

In some parts of our country, freezing water pipes are a regular winter hazard. With your family do the following:

1. Determine where water enters your home and how you turn it off. Are there separate cutoffs for the kitchen? The bathroom? The basement?

2. Practice turning the water off and on. Discuss what to do if the toilet overflows or if a sink backs up. Write the instructions in your notebook.

3. If you live in an apartment, whom do you call if you have a water emergency or find that someone else in the building has a problem. What do you do if a neighbor is not home and you

know there is a water problem because it is leaking into *your* apartment?

Now add these items to your kit for emergency use:

1. Fire extinguisher (one or more). It is always wise to have one in the kitchen as well as an extra one with the home emergency kit. You should read the instructions in detail, discuss them with your parents, then write your version in your notebook. That will help you remember. It also means that you can keep one set with the fire extinguisher, and have another, should one get lost.

2. Battery-powered radio or television set to be able to monitor bad weather situations that might leave you without any other communication. The battery-powered TV is undoubtedly a greater expense, but bad weather reports are more frequently given on television. The best radio to have is one with a weather channel.

3. Two or more battery-powered lights for use when your electricity is out. We recommend the type that can be held but also has a rack to stand on. Many camping goods stores have good lights that can almost light up a small room. A hand-held flashlight is also a must. None of these are any help if your batteries are dead, so put dates on your family self-care calendar for checking your batteries or even automatically adding new batteries. Try using each of your emergency tools.

Special Note: We strongly advise against the use of candles as they are a high-risk fire hazard. However, you should have one or two on hand just in case batteries are dead and all electricity is out for an extended time. If you must use a candle, hold it in your hand and use it only when absolutely necessary. Never leave a lighted candle burning as it can fall over and start a fire. (Family pets can also cause accidents with candles by knocking them over.)

4. Place a copy of your emergency phone numbers in your notebook. Leave this notebook in your home emergency kit.

HOME EMERGENCIES

As you know that an emergency is a situation that you must respond to immediately, let's look at those most likely to happen to *you* — home emergencies.

FIRE: THE FOUR STEPS TO SAFETY

The Number One safety worry that parents have is fire in the home. And with good reason — nearly a third of all fire victims are children! Very few grown-ups have not had to deal with a fire while they were children, or even as adults. That is why the safety rules you will learn for fires are so important that all the information should be shared by your entire family.

Step 1: What to Do When a Fire Starts

1. Leave your home or apartment immediately. If you have brothers or sisters at home, try to take them with you.
2. Call the fire department to give them your name, address, and directions to your home, and wait for instructions from them. If you are unable to remember that phone number, you can call 911 or you can dial 0 and ask the operator to call the fire department.
3. Call your parents.

Special Note: These are the three rules to *always* remember: Leave the house immediately, call the fire department, then call your parents.

Now, here are more rules for good fire safety:

4. If you live in an apartment, leave your door unlocked but closed as you leave. This means the fire will be contained in your apartment but the firemen will still be able to get in easily.

5. If you have younger brothers or sisters, keep a close eye on them so they do not try to return to your home for favorite toys or pets.

6. If you are in a room in your home and sense there is a fire outside your closed door, touch the door before opening it. If it is hot, *do not open the door*, but try to leave through another door or window if possible. If you are trapped in that room, stuff a towel or clothing under the door to keep the smoke from coming in, then open the window and shout for help.

7. If you must leave through a smoke-filled room, remember that smoke rises to the ceiling, so crawling and breathing close to the floor will be safest.

8. If your clothing catches fire, drop to the floor or ground and roll around to put the fire out.

9. If someone else's clothing catches fire, help the person roll around or grab a blanket or rug to wrap around the person and smother the fire.

10. Put out only small, contained fires yourself. Never throw water on a grease or electrical fire. Because it is often hard to know what kind of a fire you are dealing with, a good rule is to *always use a fire extinguisher on small fires.*

11. Never try to put out a fire in a bed, sofa, or couch. Leave your house immediately.

12. Install a smoke alarm in your home.

13. Place fire extinguishers in rooms where fires are most likely — the kitchen, the basement, other rooms with fireplaces and potential hazards.

Step 2: How a Fire Can Happen

Michelle, age 12, was working on her Mother's Day present for her mom. She wanted it to be a secret, so she kept everything hidden under her bed. One afternoon, just before it was time for her mother to get home from work, Michelle decided to test the present to be sure it would be as nice as she hoped.

Her present was a set of candles specially made to float in a pretty bowl. Michelle filled the bowl with water and set it on her bed. Then she locked her bedroom door so her mother wouldn't get home early, walk in, and ruin the surprise. Even though Michelle had always promised never to light matches or play with fire, she wasn't even thinking about that as she placed each candle afloat in the bowl. As she lit each one, she was pleased to see that the present was really beautiful.

In fact, Michelle was so pleased with her present, she sat down on the bed to look at it closer. But the bed was soft, the bowl tipped, and the flaming candles spilled onto her blanket. The blanket caught fire! Michelle dumped the water from the bowl onto the burning blanket and candles but it didn't help. She ran to the locked door, and panicked when she couldn't get it to open. Finally, she turned the lock and dashed into the hall. She remembered from her family's fire drill to close the door behind her.

Michelle ran out of the house and across the street to a neighbor's house, shouting "fire, fire." The neighbor heard her and had already called 911 by the time Michelle ran into the kitchen. The fire truck arrived three minutes later.

Michelle's bed was burned and most of her clothes and toys were ruined by the smoke in her bedroom. Michelle felt terrible. When her mother finally got home, poor Michelle could only cry, and the neighbor had to tell her mother how the fire had started. Michelle's mother put her arms around her, "Please, honey," she said. "You made a mistake, but you did the right thing—you remembered to close the door so our whole house didn't burn down! And you're safe! That's the best Mother's Day present. These things will happen. As long as you and I can be ready to do the right thing, that's most important."

Rob, age 14, had an experience with a fire in his home that happened in spite of the fact that his family had taken every precaution and gone through every fire drill.

It was a sunny winter afternoon. Rob was home alone as it was a school holiday and no classes were held that day. He noticed that it was getting darker outside and finally heard the sound of rain. Soon the sound grew louder. The rain turned to sleet. Rob's mother called from work. She'd heard that an ice storm was on its way and she might not be able to drive home at the usual time. She told Rob to keep an eye on the weather reports and said that she would check back with him.

Rob turned on their television set. Suddenly, the reception went out. He looked out of a window and saw that the cable line for their house had been hit by a tree limb. As he watched, the ice made more branches fall. Soon there was a constant crashing noise all around the house. Rob, feeling frightened, called his mother at her office.

"Gee, Rob," she said, "It isn't that bad here. Can you turn on the radio for a report?" Rob tried but their radio didn't offer an update.

Then he saw something really frightening — a ball of fire was bouncing on the power line that ran from Rob's house to the neighbors'. Tree branches bumping against the wire were causing it to burst into balls of flame. Rob dashed to the phone and called the fire department. He told the man who answered what he could see, then he told him his name, address, and phone number. The man asked Rob to stay on the phone with him.

"I'm going to put you on 'hold'," he said, "we want to clear this emergency line but keep in touch with you — wait ten seconds." Rob held the phone and the man was back on very quickly.

"Now, Rob," he said, "we are worried about open fires all over the city because of this storm. I want you to know that the electric company is trying to shut off the power in neighborhoods where there is danger of fire. It is going to take a little while for them to locate your block so you and I will stay on the phone until they do. Just relax and tell me if anything else happens.

Just that moment Rob saw a fire closer to their house, so close he was afraid it would ignite the roof. "All right, Rob," said the man from the fire department, "I've told a truck to get to your house. They'll be there any minute." They were! Two firemen rushed in and ran right to the box with the circuit breakers. The others ran to the side of the house where the damaged line was connected. In less than a minute, the power was off and the fire was out.

"Are you okay, son?" asked the man on the phone. Rob assured him he was. "Now don't hesitate to call back if anything else happens," said the man. "These storms are dangerous, but you should be fine with the power off."

Rob's mother wasn't able to get home until late that evening. Even though he had to sit in the dark waiting for her, Rob felt safe. He knew he could call the fire department, or even the police, if he had to.

Special Note: What if Rob's phone hadn't worked? *Then, he should have left immediately and gone to a neighbor for help.*

Step 3: Let's Imagine

How might a fire occur in your home? Let's begin by drawing a map of your home on the blank pages included here. First, draw an outline of each level or floor. Then,

1. Draw each room in your home, including closets.
2. Draw each door and window.
3. With a dotted red line, show how you would escape from each room.

Escape Route Map

Escape Route Map

4. If you live in an apartment, also draw your building with entrances, exits, and fire routes.

   Are there rooms from which it might be difficult to get out?
   Is there a phone in a room that is difficult to leave?
   Can your windows all be opened in case of emergency?
   Do you have any doors that are kept locked?
   Do you have emergency ladders for second-story windows?
   Many department and hardware stores have a variety of soft, storable ladders for this kind of use.

5. Mark with an "X" all the fire hazards you can find in each room. Walk through the room with this page in your hands so you can look around; don't rely on your memory.

   With your mom or dad, look for the following:

- Electrical outlets with more than two plugs
- Stacks of magazines or newspapers
- Curtains hanging close to a stove, heater or fireplace
- Improperly vented clothes dryer; check to see if the lint screen is working
- Matches too easily reached by young children
- Fire extinguishers several years old that may be ineffective
- Fireplace without a good screen or door
- Worn electrical wiring or cords
- Smoke alarms that have dead batteries
- Containers of flammable liquids such as gasoline, kerosene, oil
- Other dangerous liquids such as paint, paint thinner, varnish
- Cleaning fluids, lighter fluid
- Greasy areas around the kitchen stove such as the hood right above it or the areas just beneath the burners where food can catch fire. Do you have a family system for checking to be sure that anyone who uses the stove *turns it off*?
- List here other hazards you find:

Discuss this list with your family. Be sure you are aware of potential problem areas.

If you live in an apartment, be sure to mark on your Building page all the escape routes for your building, including routes from other apartments where you may visit. Note, too, your trash collection areas and the locations of furnaces or other areas where fires might start. Mark the location of your building's fire extinguishers and stop to read all directions.

Special Note: If you live in an apartment and there is a fire in your building, use the stairs for an escape route; never use the elevators.

Step 4: Practice

Ask your mom or dad to observe you doing the following:

1. Pretend that there is a fire in each room of your house. Give the reason the fire started, tell how you found it, and tell what you will do about it.

   Lower Level or Basement

   Main Floor

   Upstairs

   Garage

   Building

Now you know the first steps to take if there is a fire. The practice alone will help you to know, almost without thinking, what to do first.

2. Plan a fire drill that includes a phone call to an emergency number. All members of your family should participate. Set a time, every two or three months, for everyone to take turns calling a surprise fire drill, just like those at school. If your parents are too busy to do this, practice with a friend; have one at your house, then one at your friend's house.

3. Practice locating the gas, electrical, and water cutoffs quickly.

4. Consider what would happen if an emergency occurred and you didn't have what you need. For example, what would you do if you didn't have a flashlight in a power outage?

If someone you know is on fire and there is no rug or blanket to wrap around them, what could you use? Your coat? A curtain?

STORMS: THE FOUR STEPS TO SAFETY

Storms — tornados, hurricanes, snowstorms, and severe thunderstorms — can be very frightening if you are home alone. They are among the more common causes of home emergencies such as fire and flooding.

The safety rules for preparing for a tornado are good guidelines to follow for almost any storm situation.

Step 1: What to Do

1. When you hear the warning sounded or you are alerted in other ways, turn on a battery-powered radio or TV in order to be able to hear the weather bulletins.

2. In case of immediate danger, move quickly to a room below ground level, such as a basement, where you should keep close to inside walls. If you do not have a basement, seek cover in a closet, under a table or a bed, or in a bathtub with a mattress over you. Be sure to stay away from any windows or doors that might have flying glass.

Mobile homes are specially vulnerable. In a tornado, you should evacuate and try to find a more permanent shelter, or lie flat in a ditch or on the ground with something covering you.

Flooding can occur long after a storm is over. Young people are often playing around streams or bridges when flash floods suddenly hit. Do you have flash flooding in your area? Are there places where you should not play before or after stormy weather?

3. Call your mom or dad before or after the storm, depending on your family's self-care rules.

Step 2: How It Can Happen

Rob's story earlier in this chapter is an excellent example of the kind of home emergency that can occur because of storms. Did you notice that the emergency was not Rob's fault in any way? Because his family was prepared, he was able to get help immediately.

However, he *was* able to use the phone. What would you have done if the phone didn't work? Would you leave the house immediately? Where would you go?

Step 3: Let's Imagine

List here the kinds of storms and storm hazards you have in your area:

Step 4: Practice

Discuss with your family what to do in a bad storm:

Whom do you call? _____

How do you prepare your home? _____

Where do you take cover? _____

What do you do with family pets? _____

HOME ALONE

An important part of self-care is going and coming from your family's home all by yourself. You need to know just what to do each time you leave, and each time you return. You need to know safe ways to handle the keys to your home, as well as locks, lights, and the yard.

Your Key

With your parents, decide how many keys you will need. Will you need just one for the front door? Do you live in an apartment and need a key for the main entrance, too?

Make extra copies of your key. Now decide how to carry it safely. Should you wear it on a string around your neck and tucked into your clothing? Do you want it on a key ring and slipped into your pocket or a purse? Where will you keep it when you are home? Is there a special dish or box to hold your key? Do you need to mark your key?

Special Note: Never give your key to someone else — not even a good friend at school. You might forget that your friend has it, and find yourself locked out. Never give your key to anyone!

Find places to keep extra keys in case you forget yours someday. Work with your parents to decide this. Remember, you should never hide a key outdoors; too many people are able to find hidden keys. Instead, decide on neighbors and friends who will be good key keepers. One or two may live close by, but one might also be someone who can be called in an emergency, even though the friend doesn't live close by. Perhaps you have a friendly store-owner in your neighborhood whom you know well and who would be happy to keep an emergency key for you.

Write the names and addresses of your key keepers here:

Locks

Keys fit into locks, of course. Check your locks. Do they all work? Ask your parents to be sure that your home has the kind of locks that will protect you.

List your locks and their locations here:

Lights

Having a lot of light in and around your home often helps you feel much safer when you are home alone — especially good outdoor lights if you live in a house. Ask your parents to help you check to see if all your lights, indoors and outdoors, are working.

List here the lights to turn on as it gets dark:

Yard

Do you have a lot of bushes and trees around your house or your building? Can these be trimmed so you feel safe walking home alone? Is there a way to walk up to your door that makes you feel safe and comfortable coming home?

Coming and Going

List here all the things to check before you walk out the door:

Key? _____

Things to turn off _____

Things to turn on _____

Pets to let in or out _____

Other _____

Now list all the things to check before you walk *in* the door:

How should our home look from the outside?

What signs might mean that something is wrong?

What do I do if I see an open door or window?

Think about this: Our pet is outside even though no one is home . . . an unusual light is turned on . . . a strange car is in the driveway . . . other signs?

What do I do if I see any of these signs?

EMERGENCY ARRIVAL PLAN

Now work with your parents to plan what you should do when things don't look right:

1. Make an emergency phone call. Where will I go to make this call — to a neighbor's home? A friend? The superintendent of our building? _____

2. Whom do I call first? The police? Mom or Dad? _____

3. Follow the directions of the person you called.

4. Wait for help.

Please remember: Do not *ever* feel too embarrassed to call for help even if you are not sure if anything is wrong! A very important thing for you to do in self-care is to be able to judge when something *might* be wrong.

If the police come to help you, but no one is in your home, that's all right! They want to help you feel safe. Maybe the wind blew the door open that day. The policemen and policewomen have children, too. They are happy to help you feel safe. Don't ever hesitate to go for help if your home doesn't look right from the outside!

SCARY NOISES

What if you are home alone and you begin to hear strange noises? First, work with your parents to learn how to judge these noises. Often, when you are home alone, noises can be frightening even though they are not signs of danger.

The Noise Test

Before you begin self-care, you and your family should spend an evening home with no television, radio, or record players on so you learn the sounds of all the noises in your home.

Make a list of familiar noises here:

Does your furnace or hot water heater make noise? _____

Do your basement or stairs creak _____

Does your chimney whistle? _____

Does your next-door neighbor come home late and slam doors? _____

What other noises do you hear? _____

Now that you are familiar with your home's noises, you will be better able to judge whether or not you hear dangerous ones.

Special Note: Even if you know noises are okay, they may still make you feel frightened or nervous. It often helps to turn your television up loud enough so you can't hear them.

HOME ALONE: THE FOUR STEPS TO SAFETY

"I hear noises — someone is breaking into our house!"

The worst has happened; you are sure the noises mean danger. Let's look at what you should think about now.

Step 1: What to Do

1. Go to your neighbor's or friend's — the place that you and your parents have chosen for making emergency phone calls. Do not stay at home or close to your home.
2. If you can reach your mom or dad easily, call them so they know, too.
3. Call 911 or the police and say "I think someone has broken into my home. I am (your name), I'm (your age) and I'm home alone. Can you help me?" Now give the police your address and directions to your house.
4. Wait for the police to help you.

Even if you are wrong and there is no one in your home when the police get there, don't worry and don't be embarrassed; you need to feel safe.

Step 2: How It Can Happen

It was a cold, wintry Thursday afternoon and Ryan, age eleven, was home from school. He and his mother and stepfather lived in a little ranch house with their two cats. Ryan was relaxing in front of the TV when he suddenly heard a pounding noise.

He wasn't frightened, as it was still daytime — about four o'clock in the afternoon.

He looked through the front windows where he could see if anyone was at the door, but no one was there. Now the pounding was louder. He looked out of the windows again, but this time he could see a van in the driveway. As it was very cold, the windows were clouded up and he couldn't see very well. He could not see the faces of the people in the van.

Ryan was scared. He didn't know anyone who drove a van. He ran to the telephone. He called his mother at work. "Mom, Mom, someone is trying to crash into our house!"

Ryan's mother was surprised. "What do you mean?" she asked.

"A big red van is in our driveway and bumping up against the garage door," said Ryan. He could feel himself almost ready to cry.

"Do you think it's friends of your big brother?" his mother asked, trying to calm him down.

"No," said Ryan, "I've never seen this red van before!"

"All right," said Ryan's mother. "Hang up. I'll call 911. Then I'll call you back."

Ryan hung up. He could feel himself shaking now and the pounding was louder. His mom was very worried, too. As she dialed 911, she thought about how good and responsible Ryan had been in self-care. This was the first time he'd ever been frightened.

"Hello," she said to the 911 operator. "My son Ryan is home alone. He's only eleven years old and someone in a large van is trying to crash into our garage door. Our address is 4600 West 23rd Street."

"We'll have someone right there," said the 911 operator.

Ryan's mother called him. "They're on their way, honey," she said. "Now I'll stay on the phone with you until the police get there."

They waited less than a minute before Ryan heard the siren and saw the police car drive up. A policeman jumped out and ran up to the van. He pulled open the door, and out stepped Ryan's big brother.

"Thank goodness," said Ryan's mother. "I'm glad it's not strangers, but, boy, am I angry with him. You tell him to call me right away," she said to Ryan.

What had happened? Why would Ryan's big brother do something like this? The van wasn't hitting the garage door, but the big boys were horsing around inside and pounding the walls of the van. They thought they were having fun together, but Ryan heard the pounding and thought — as he couldn't see very well from the house — that the van was hitting the house.

"I am very angry with you and your friends," said Ryan's mother to his big brother. "You must remember that Ryan is all by himself. Please be extra careful to let him know that you are coming in the house or having friends over. If you are arriving in a different car, try to wave right away so he knows you are not a stranger."

The policeman assured Ryan that everything was all right. He told his big brother to be more careful and not to horse around so much. Then he patted Ryan on the shoulder before he left.

Step 3: Let's Imagine

Ask your parents to talk with you about your home and the homes around you. Do your neighbors have intruders or burglars very often? If they do, you and your parents may want to arrange a special safety check if you are going to be home alone at times that break-ins are most likely to occur.

After talking with your parents about the kinds of noises — normal or dangerous — that you might hear in your home, write a short story for yourself. Your story should be about a noise you heard and what you did after you heard it.

Here is space for your story:

Step 4: Practice

1. Look over your list of noises. Review these with your parents so they know what worries you and you have a better idea of what the scary but normal noises are.

2. Look again at Chapter Five, "Physical Safety." Now have your parents or a friend listen and watch while you pretend that you hear a frightening noise and act out all the things you should do. Practice placing a call to 911 or the police. Be sure you give all the information they would need in order to help you.

3. Check your house rules with your parents and discuss how you will answer — or not answer — the door if a stranger knocks or rings your doorbell.

   If you are under age ten, your mom or dad may say that you should not answer the door. They may want you to call them or another adult so someone knows that a stranger is at your door.

   If you are over age ten, it may be all right to answer the door. However, can you see who is there before you open the door? Does your home have a peephole in the door or a good window you can use? Can you keep your screen door locked? If not, what can you do to be sure you know who is at the door *before* you answer? _____

   _____

Special Note: Never tell a stranger that your mom and dad aren't home. Simply say that they are busy and cannot come to the door now. Then call your mom or dad.

Write here the house rule that your family wants everyone to follow when strangers come to your home and you are alone:

Write here the house rule your family will follow when people are supposed to come to your house when you are home alone. For example, how will your parents arrange for repairmen to come? Be sure your rule includes:

1. Telling you ahead of time that a visitor is expected.
2. Providing for some kind of identification of the visitor — a badge, uniform, the visitor's name, a phone call before the visitor arrives.

7
YOUR NEIGHBORHOOD

If you are going to have a good self-care plan, you and your parents need to be sure that you know your neighborhood well. You must know directions to and from home, safe and dangerous areas, homes of people who can help you, and different kinds of transportation you can use.

Let's begin by drawing a map of your neighborhood on the blank pages included here.

1. Draw the entire area around your home where you are allowed to go by yourself. Mark your home with a large red "X." Label the streets in your neighborhood.

2. Mark all the places you are allowed to go—school, church, classes, friend's homes.

3. Mark your playgrounds, library, shops where you are allowed to run errands.

4. With a dotted line, draw the route you take from home to the places you go most often, such as your school.

5. With your parents, mark those areas you know are dangerous, or where your parents do not want you to be by yourself.

6. If you have block mothers in your neighborhood, mark the locations of those homes. These families have signs in their windows that say "block mother" so you know you can always knock on their doors if you need help of any kind.

My Neighborhood

My Neighborhood

7. Mark the telephones you can use. Be sure to mark pay telephone locations as well as the homes of friends and neighbors who will let you use a telephone.

8. Mark those areas of your neighborhood where you worry about getting lost.

9. Mark those areas where you worry about seeing people who may hurt you.

10. Do you have other special places to mark in your neighborhood? List them here:

Getting Around

Now list all the different kinds of transportation you can use in your neighborhood. Include phone numbers whenever possible. Also, add those phone numbers to your family phone list that you keep available for emergencies.

Cabs _____

Buses _____

Subways _____

Friends _____

Other _____

Late Plans

What will you do if you miss your bus after school or after your piano lesson? Is there another kind of transportation you can use? Should you call someone? Write your late plan here:

If you are late and it is beginning to get dark, are there areas of your neighborhood where you should not walk? Discuss these with your mom or dad and list them here:

Who are all your friends and neighbors who can help you if you have an emergency when you are out alone in your neighborhood? Write their names and phone numbers here:

Now answer these questions and ask your parents to check your answers:

Do I feel safe in my neighborhood?

If not, which areas worry me?

Which are the safe areas?

Can I get from one place to another easily?

If I have to go somewhere after dark, am I often frightened?

Can I get home easily, if I get out of school or a class late?

What is the best kind of transportation for me to use?

Do I worry about getting lost?

Are there people in my neighborhood who frighten me? Who are they?

MY NEIGHBORHOOD AND DANGER

We like to think that our neighborhoods are safe. Most of the time they are, but everyone should know that dangerous things can happen anywhere. If you know the kind of thing that can happen, and what you should do if it happens to you, you will feel much safer whenever you are out.

Be sure to read about these dangers. They will probably never happen to you, but you want to be prepared, especially if you are in self-care.

Strangers

Strangers are people whom you don't know. They can be good, kind people. They can be dangerous. They can be men or women, boys or girls. They can look dangerous or they can look very safe. Remember, *if you do not know a person, you must never go anywhere with the person, give your name or address, or tell the person that you are alone.*

Work with your parents to decide what to do in the following situations.

1. If a stranger asks you for help or directions, what should you say?

   Some families decide that the best answer is "I'm sorry, I can't help you." Then leave quickly. If you are still worried, stop and call for help as soon as you can.

2. If a stranger follows you on the street, where should you go? To a friend's house? Into a store?

Find a safe place as soon as you can. Look for a block mother's home. Go to a store or a gas station and tell an adult that you are being followed. Never be embarrassed to ask for help.

3. If a stranger keeps bothering you, what should you do?

Drug addicts, drunks, and crazy people can be frightening. Never hesitate to run away and ask for help if you are being bothered.

4. Discuss with your parents what kinds of strangers you will find in your neighborhood. List them here:

Mugging and Assault

Many children, whether their parents are home or if they are in self-care, have to worry at times about mugging and assault. This means being robbed or beaten up. The attacker can be an adult or another child. Sometimes, older children and teenagers pick on younger children. They may try to steal their lunch money or their bus pass. They may just want to be mean.

Here are some ways you can protect yourself from mugging and assault. Talk these over with your mom and dad.

1. Always keep a safe distance from other people when you are on the street or in a bus or subway. If you notice that someone is getting too close to you, move away.

2. Think about looking busy. Even if you are afraid, keep a determined look on your face as if you know just what you are doing. Avoid staring at people or looking them in the eye. Sometimes, just avoiding eye contact can make a difference; you don't give the other person a chance to bother you.

3. Always try to walk with other children, especially after dark. It is safer to spend money on a cab than to walk home alone in many neighborhoods. Talk with your parents about your neighborhood after dark. Whom can you call if you are alone and worried about how to get home?

4. Always pay attention to what is happening around you when you are on the street. Is there a drunk staggering toward you? Is there a person behaving strangely near your bus stop? Don't get so involved with your friends that you don't pay attention to the people around you.

Special Note: When you are on the street, if you are prepared and aware, you will feel safe *because you will know how and when to get help.* This is part of growing up and becoming independent.

Here are some things Mom and Dad should do if you are mugged or assaulted.

1. Check for physical injury. Don't blame your child. Reassurance is needed right now.
2. Watch for symptoms that your child is very worried about this experience. Symptoms to watch for include sleeplessness, loss of appetite, and depression. If your child is unable to forget what happened, seek professional help.
3. Do not become overprotective. Take steps to avoid this happening again such as making sure your child doesn't walk alone, but stays with companions.
4. Be sure your child knows that he or she did not cause the incident.
5. Discuss ways to get help or stay safe with your child. Practice these several times so your child can react quickly even when frightened. Consider enrolling your child in a self-defense class, especially if there is a constant threat in your neighborhood.
6. If the threat is constant, perhaps you can work with other parents to provide a safety system such as parent patrols or group activities that will keep your child off the street.

Sexual Assault

Sexual assault is a serious problem, whether you are a child or a parent. It is very important to know that most children who are sexually abused, are abused by people they know such as family members or friends.

First, you should talk about sexual assault as a family. What is it? Have you seen stories in the newspaper recently that tell about sexual abuse? List here some examples of sexual assault that you have heard about:

Because children in self-care are particularly susceptible to sexual assault, we are placing a special emphasis on these guidelines. Please read them and discuss them as a family.

For Children: How to Protect Yourself from Sexual Assault

1. No adult or older child has the right to force or trick you into sexual contact.
2. If someone touches you in ways that make you uncomfortable, tell your mom or dad—even if the person threatens to hurt you. The person could be someone you know and like. It may be confusing and very difficult to tell someone, but *you must get help.*
3. If your mom or dad won't believe you, keep telling people until someone does. Tell other relatives, your minister, or anyone you trust. You must get help.
4. Sexual assault is not your fault. Don't ever feel that it is.

For Parents—The Signals of Sexual Assault

1. Genital trauma, soreness, or infection.
2. Physical complaints such as headaches, stomachaches, and constipation.
3. Signs of stress such as sleeplessness or poor performance in school.
4. Reluctance to stay home with a brother or sister; go shopping with a friend or relative; spend time with a particular person.
5. Overattachment to a friend or relative. Inappropriate touching of another person.
6. "Acting out" sexually with others.
7. A report from your child that he or she is being abused.

Special note: Be aware of these facts about sexual assault:

1. Sexual assault can be perpetrated by a person of the same sex as your child.
2. Boys are assaulted as often as girls.
3. The child molester is not easily categorized by personal profile, income, or class level.

Kidnapping

Stealing children is a terrible crime. It doesn't happen very often, but it is a danger to be aware of every time you are on the street by yourself. This makes it very important to avoid strangers and follow all your family rules for taking care of yourself in your neighborhood.

NEIGHBORHOOD DANGER: THE FOUR STEPS TO SAFETY

Step 1: What to Do

1. Write the stranger rules for your family's self-care agreement, using the guidelines included in this chapter.
2. Check your telephone rules to be sure you know whom to call if you have a problem with a stranger in your home or in your neighborhood.
3. Complete the map of your neighborhood and be sure your parents know what worries you. You should also be aware of their concerns.
4. Will you be caring for younger brothers or sisters? Ask your parents to be sure to talk with them about the stranger rules. Be sure your parents tell the younger children all about strangers. It won't be good if you know all about strangers, but they don't, because they may be the ones approached some day. Be sure they understand why you have rules about where they can play in your neighborhood.
5. If you have younger brothers and sisters, even if you are not in charge, plan a warning signal so that you can warn one another if there is a danger around you. For example, plan to say "Hey, time to scram" or "Jeff, mother is calling" to alert your brother or sister to a danger they may not see.

Step 2: How It Can Happen

One bright sunny day, Jeff, age ten, was walking home from school with his friends, when they heard police sirens coming their way. The boys stopped at the corner, just a half-block from Jeff's house, and watched a bright red Corvette come speeding toward them with four police cars right behind.

"Watch out, Jeff!" shouted Carrie. She pushed Jeff away from the street just as the red car suddenly spun around, crashed into a telephone pole, and jumped over the curb onto the lawn of the house right across the street from Jeff's house.

Jeff ran across the street to his house just as the police cars stopped and the police jumped out. The man in the red car had jumped out, too. He ran towards Jeff's house, stopped, and turned to run down the street in the other direction. The police saw him. They pulled out their guns and ran after him. Jeff followed.

"Jeff, don't go!" shouted Carrie again. "I'll tell your mom." Carrie started to cry but Jeff just hollered, "Hey, I wanna see what happens." He stopped and watched as the police caught the man, put handcuffs on him, and put him in the back of the police car.

While all of this was going on, Jeff's mom was on her way home from the office. This had been her first week at a new job, and she was feeling happy. The people were nice, her office was only ten minutes away from the house where she and Jeff lived, and Jeff could walk to school. Their neighborhood was nice, with lots of trees and grass and very friendly people. Jeff knew where the block mother's house was, and they also had a cute dog to help Jeff feel safe when he was alone.

"We're so lucky; everything seems so safe," Jeff's mom thought to herself. Just then she turned the corner toward their house—and almost ran into a police car! Two police cars were in their driveway, and two more were in the middle of the street. Across from her house was a bright red Corvette with the engine still running—parked in the center of Mrs. Larson's lawn.

Jeff stood on the sidewalk watching the police. "Hey, Mom," he shouted when he saw her. "The police just caught a bad guy; I saw it all. Wow! They had guns and everything."

"Jeff," said his mother. "Get in the house—right now." She felt herself start to shake. Jeff saw how frightened his mother looked.

"It's okay," he said. "They caught him; I saw it. . . ."

"Jeffrey!"

Why do you think Jeff's mom was upset?

He did not follow any of the rules they had discussed for Jeff's self-care. Jeff's mom sat him down that afternoon and explained to him what could have happened: the car might have run right into Jeff and his friends; the police might have had to use their guns and might have accidentally shot someone standing around; or the man might have tried to grab someone like Jeff to use as a hostage.

"We have a good neighborhood," said Jeff's mom to him, "but it is only as safe as you and I make it by following the rules. What should you have done today instead of running after the police?"

"Well," said Jeff. "First, when we heard the sirens, we should have stopped, moved far away from the street, and made sure none of the little kids got too close."

"Good," said his mom. "What else?"

"I think that when all the cars stopped and the man jumped out, we should have run back to school."

"Right," said his mom, "or you should have gone next door to Mrs. Jordan's house. You know she expects you to go there when you have an emergency. Then, you should have called me right away. If I had known about this today, I would have left the office an hour ago! You must tell me right away when things happen."

"I'm really sorry, Mom," said Jeff. "I didn't think; it was just like TV."

"You don't get hurt by TV stuff," said his mom. "You might have been hurt today." Then she gave Jeff a big hug. "I love you too much to want to take chances. This is a good lesson for both of us; bad things can happen anywhere. So let's be very careful; okay?" "You be careful, too, Mom," Jeff said and hugged her.

Step 3: Let's Imagine

1. Think of some strange or frightening people you might see in your neighborhood. Ask your parents if they have seen any people that you should be sure to avoid.

2. Think of danger spots in your area that you should avoid. Tell your parents about them. Have your parents tell you the danger spots they worry about.

3. Think of a story about a stranger coming up to a child. Tell this story to your mom or dad. Think of all the things the stranger might say to try to persuade the child to go with the stranger. Think of what the child can do to get away.

Step 4: Practice

1. Ask your parent or a friend to pretend to be a dangerous person. Practice all the things you should do so this person cannot hurt you.

2. Practice using a pay telephone to make a call for help to get away from a person who frightens you.

3. Pretend that you are the bad person; what do you think will be a very clever way to try to trick a child?

4. Now answer these questions and ask your mom or dad to check your answers:

You are walking down the street and an old woman in a car asks you to come over and see her new kitten. What should you do?

You are walking home after the basketball game and a carload of teenagers pulls up next to you on the street. They start shouting at you. What should you do?

What are the best things a stranger could offer you? A trip to Disney World? A movie? A new bike?

If you are playing with younger children and a stranger comes up and starts talking to one of them, what should you do? How can you get the other children away from the stranger?

If you are going to school with your younger sister, and an older boy in a car grabs her, what should you do? (*Hint:* Go for help but also try to remember the license number of the car. Remember, you are probably not strong enough to help your sister, but you can tell the police the facts about the person and the car. Look for the things that will identify the person: color of hair and eyes, kind of clothing, whether or not you have seen this person before.)

How can you tell a dangerous stranger from one who will not hurt you? (*Hint:* Such a person will approach you when you are alone and do not have an adult to help you. This person will often try to offer you a treat in order to get you to go somewhere.)

What if a stranger acted as if you did something wrong and told you to get in his or her car "right now." What should you do?

What if someone you don't know comes to your school and wants to take you home? What should you do?

What if a pleasant woman told you that you looked so cute, you should be in the movies, and she wanted to help you? What should you do?

Do you feel safe in your neighborhood? If not, what can you and your parents do to make you feel better?

8

YOUR SELF

You are a very important person — to your parents, to the people around you and, of course, to yourself. That is why knowing how to take care of yourself if you get sick or hurt while you're home alone is essential to a good self-care plan. This chapter will teach you many ways of knowing whether or not you are sick enough to need a doctor.

FEELING SICK

The worst thing about feeling sick in self-care is that your mom or dad can't be there with you. However, we are going to give you some ways to think about your sickness so both you and your parents will be able to judge how serious it is even though you are talking by phone and they can't see you.

In fact, since many children in self-care get sick after a parent has left home—during the school day or after school—we think that the following questions should be copied for your mom and dad to have at the office, too. That way they will know just what to ask you in order to tell if they need to come home to help.

First, ask your parents what you should do if you need to see a doctor right away but your parents cannot be reached. Write the answer on the next page.

The most common illnesses you are likely to experience while you are in self-care are the ones we will discuss here: headaches, stomachaches, vomiting, diarrhea, colds, sore throats, coughs, earaches, and fevers.

Call Dr. _____

at _____

Call these numbers for medical emergencies:

_____   _____

_____   _____

_____   _____

Now, discuss these questions with your parents, so you know what to think about when you are sick.

How Bad Is My Headache?

If you answer "yes" to any of these questions, your parents should call a doctor immediately:

1. Were you hit in the head before getting the headache?
2. Is the pain so bad that you feel you can't move your head without crying or screaming?
3. Do other people think you seem confused or find it hard to wake you up?
4. Is your vision blurred or do you see double?
5. Is it hard for you to walk?
6. Have you vomited three or more times?
7. Is it hard for you to touch your chin to the center of your chest?

If you answer "yes" to any of these questions, your parents should call a doctor during office hours:

1. Are headaches a regular problem for you?
2. Do you have pain on just one side?
3. Do you have other things wrong with you, such as a bad cold?

4. Have you had your headache longer than twelve hours even after taking aspirin?

5. Has your headache been getting worse?

If you know that you do not need to see a doctor, here are some ways to help yourself feel better.

1. Lie down and rest.
2. With permission from your mom or dad, take the pain medication they recommend.
3. Put a cool washcloth on your forehead.
4. If something is bothering you, talk it over with your mom and dad as soon as possible.

How Bad Is My Stomachache?

If you answer "yes" to any of these questions, your parents should call a doctor immediately:

1. Is the pain so severe that it makes you cry or scream? Is it getting worse?
2. When you walk, do you have to bend over or hold your stomach?
3. Have you had blood in your bowel movement?
4. Could you have been poisoned with someone's medicine or a chemical?
5. Have you had an injury to your stomach?
6. Gently press on your stomach in different spots, then tell your parents how you respond. Is there a definite tenderness in any spot, especially in your lower right side or near your groin?
7. Have you had the pain more than two hours?
8. Does it burn when you urinate?

If you answer "yes" to any of the following questions, your parents should call your doctor during office hours because your stomachache may be part of another problem.

1. Do you have cramps from constipation? (If you have diarrhea or are vomiting, read the guidelines under those sections, which follow in this chapter.)

2. Have you been coughing hard?
3. Do you have a sore throat?
4. Are you having your menstrual period?
5. Do you often have stomachaches?

If you do not need to see a doctor, here are some ways to feel better:

1. Lie down and rest.
2. Put a warm washcloth on your stomach.
3. Sip some clear fluids such as water or ginger ale.
4. Keep a pan handy in case you need to vomit.
5. Don't take any medicine.

What if I'm Vomiting?

If you answer "yes" to any of these questions, your parents should call your doctor immediately:

1. Is there blood in your vomit (and it is not from a recent nosebleed)?
2. Has your stomach or abdomen been hurting for more than four hours?
3. Has it been more than twelve hours since you urinated?
4. Do you feel confused or delirious? Do you keep falling asleep and find it very hard to wake up?
5. Have you had a recent injury or blow to your stomach or abdomen?
6. Have you taken any drugs or chemicals?
7. Is it hard for you to touch your chin to the center of your chest?
8. Have you had a blow to your head within the last week?
9. Are you feeling very sick?

If you answer "yes" to any of the following questions, your parents should call a doctor during office hours.

1. Is your vomiting caused by coughing too hard?
2. Are you on medication for another problem?

3. Have you been vomiting more than two days?
4. Do you also have diarrhea?
5. Are you vomiting often?

If you do not need to see a doctor, here are some ways to feel better:

1. Do not eat any solid food or take any medication for eight hours.
2. Drink sips of clear fluids such as Gatorade, ginger ale, cola, or 7-Up (stir or shake the soda pop until the bubbles disappear). Start with just a swallow or two every twenty minutes. Double the amount each hour if you feel better and do not vomit again.
3. Keep a pan by you in case you need to vomit again.
4. After eight hours without vomiting, you can have some toast, crackers, honey on bread, a bland soup, rice, or mashed potatoes.

What if I Have Diarrhea?

If you answer "yes" to any of the following questions, your parents should call a doctor immediately:

1. Are you having diarrhea constantly, more than once an hour?
2. Have you had diarrhea more than eight times in the last eight hours?
3. Do you have blood in your diarrhea?
4. Are you also having severe stomach cramps?
5. Has it been more than twelve hours since you urinated?

If you answer "yes" to any of the following questions, your parents need to call a doctor during office hours:

1. Have you had diarrhea for more than a week?
2. Do you have mucus or pus in your diarrhea?
3. Are you also vomiting?
4. Have you had a fever of over 100° F for more than three days?
5. Are you on medication?
6. Do you have diarrhea often?

Here is a diet that can help you feel better while having diarrhea; but, most important, be *sure to drink lots of water to prevent dehydration.*

1. Do not drink any milk.
2. First Day: Saltine crackers, white toast with honey, rice, applesauce, bland soup, active-culture yogurt.
3. Second Day: Lean meats, soft-boiled eggs, noodles.
4. Third Day: Soft, cooked fruits and vegetables (pears, carrots, potatoes).
5. Fourth Day: Regular diet but no milk, ice cream, or cheese.
6. Eighth Day: Slowly add milk, ice cream, and cheese to your diet.

How Bad Is My Cold?

A cold is a runny or stuffy nose from a viral infection. If you answer "yes" to the following question, your parents should call a doctor immediately:

Is it hard for you to breathe, even when you open your mouth?

If you answer "yes" to any of the following questions, your parents should call a doctor during office hours:

1. Have you had yellow or green discharge from your nose for more than twenty-four hours?
2. Have you had clear discharge from your nose for more than a week?
3. Is there blood in the discharge from your nose that is not from a simple nosebleed?
4. Do you have a fever of over 100° F? If so, have you had it more than three days?
5. Do you have other things wrong such as a sore throat or a cough?
6. Do you have matter in your eyes; not just red eyes?

Your parents can help you feel better by using the kinds of treatment and medication that your family doctor recommends.

How Bad Is My Sore Throat, Bad Cough, or Earache?

If you answer "yes" to any of the following questions, your parents should call a doctor immediately:

Sore Throat

1. Is it very hard for you to open your mouth fully or are you drooling?
2. Is it hard for you to breathe, and you do not have a stuffy nose?
3. Is the pain so severe that you can't stand it?

Cough

Do you make a crowing, croupy sound when you cough or when you breathe?
2. Is there a wheezing sound in your chest like the purring of a cat?
3. Is your breathing very difficult or labored?
4. Have you coughed up any bloody mucus?

Earache

1. Is the pain so severe that it makes you cry or scream?
2. Have you had an injury or blow to your ear?
3. Is your neck stiff?

If you have symptoms of a sore throat, cough, or earache that are less severe, your parents will have suggestions from your family doctor than can help you feel better.

How Bad Is My Fever?

A fever is a rectal temperature of over 100.4° F or an oral temperature of over 100° F. Most children in self-care are able to take their oral temperature. However, if this is difficult, new medical products have been developed, such as a band attached to the child's forehead, that make taking the temperature a very simple task.

Everyone should know that fever is the body's normal response to viral or bacterial infections. Generally, the height of the fever does not relate to the seriousness of the illness. How sick a child acts is what counts.

If you answer "yes" to any of the following questions, your parents should call your doctor immediately:

1. Is your fever over 105° F?
2. Do you find it very difficult to wake up?
3. Do you seem confused—to yourself or to others?
4. Is your neck stiff?
5. Do you think you have had a seizure?
6. Do you have purple spots on your skin?
7. Is it hard for you to breathe even after you blow your nose?
8. Do you feel very sick?

If you answer "yes" to any of the following questions, your parents should call your doctor during office hours:

1. Is your fever between 104° and 105° F?
2. Do you have a burning sensation or pain when you urinate?
3. Have you had your fever more than six days?
4. Have you had your fever more than twenty-four hours, with no sign of the cause or location of an infection?
5. Did your fever go away for over twenty-four hours and then return?
6. Do you have a history of seizures?
7. Do you have other questions about how you feel?

Here are some ways to feel better when you have a high fever:

1. Drink lots of iced drinks. You lose body fluids while sweating, so you need the extra liquids.
2. Cover yourself lightly. If you are shivering or cold, use a light blanket, but don't bundle yourself up as that can cause your fever to go even higher.
3. Get a lot of rest. While you should avoid rigorous activity, normal activity is fine.
4. Your parents should check with your doctor to decide which fever-reducing medication is right for you. Never take your medicine more often than the instructions say. If you fall

asleep, don't wake yourself up just to take the medicine; sleep first, then take your next dose.

5. Do not take aspirin if you have the chickenpox or flu because of possible links with a dangerous disease, Reye's Syndrome.

6. If your temperature is very high, over 104° F, you can lower it by sponging. Sit in just two inches of lukewarm water and sponge yourself with a cloth. This works better than a full tub of water and is much more comfortable. Raise the water temperature if you begin to shiver.

Special Note: These questions have been based on recommendations made by Dr. Barton D. Schmitt in his excellent book, *Pediatric Telephone Advice*, Little, Brown & Co., Boston, 1980. This book was written by Dr. Schmitt to be used by pediatric physicians as they diagnose children's illnesses when speaking to parents by telephone.

If you have a significant number of health problems in your family, you may want to look for his forthcoming book for parents, which discusses nearly 200 different health problems. This book is already available on software for IBM, Tandy, and Apple home computers through Clinical Reference Systems, Inc. of Denver. The title of the software is *The Home Health Guide for Children.*

9
FIRST AID

First aid is one of the most important skills you need for good, safe self-care. If your community offers a first-aid course, you should take it before starting self-care; especially if you will be caring for younger brothers or sisters.

This chapter offers you some basic directions for first aid that you might need for yourself or others while you are home in self-care. Each first-aid action will be presented with our "Four Steps to Safety"—What to Do; How It Can Happen; Let's Imagine (How This Can Happen in Your Home); Practice.

FIRST-AID KIT

Find a good sturdy box that you will be able to keep in an easy-to-reach place. Label this "First Aid." Now work with your mom or dad to buy or find each of the following:

1. Boxes of bandaids. Look for Telfa adhesive pads—these won't stick to a scrape or cut. Also be sure to get one box of assorted sizes, and a box of two-by-three-inch pads as well for larger wounds.

2. Two rolls of gauze, sizes one-inch and two-inch.

3. One roll of one-inch adhesive tape. Include a small scissors (perhaps an old fingernail scissors) to cut this tape. Cutters attached to rolls of tape generally don't work easily.

4. One box of large sterile gauze pads.

5. An antiseptic spray or cream.

6. An extra bar of soap.
7. Tweezers for slivers.
8. A bottle of syrup of ipecac in case of poisoning.
9. Several towels or cloths for making ice packs.
10. Check with your mom or dad to see if you need anything else such as a special skin cream in case you get poison ivy easily.
11. Notebook. Read the rest of this chapter to find out what goes into this notebook.

FIRST-AID ACTION

Now, you are ready to learn some basic first-aid. As you read, write the first aid directions in your special first-aid kit notebook. Why? There are two reasons:

First, several people in your family may read and use this book so you won't always know where it is. However, if you keep your first-aid notebook with your first-aid kit, you will have it when you need it most.

Second, you always remember things better when you write them down. The directions we are going to give you are ones that you should practice and *memorize*. Write, practice, and memorize—the secret to good first aid!

PHONE AID

Begin your first-aid notebook by listing the emergency phone numbers you might need, including all the necessary phone numbers for your mom and dad.

Ask your parents these questions and write the answers here.

If I have a lot of bleeding or feel I can't breathe, should I call 911 or the police first?

If I have other emergencies, should I call you before I call for emergency help?

If I cannot reach you in an emergency, whom should I call?

MEDICAL RELEASES

Ask your parents to provide medical release forms to all the people who might need to help you in an emergency. This means that they can tell a hospital or doctor to go ahead and take care of you.

Check with your local hospital for the correct wording on your medical releases.

BLEEDING: THE FOUR STEPS TO SAFETY

Step 1: What to Do

Small Cuts and Scrapes

1. Find a clean towel or cloth or piece of paper towel and press it hard against the bleeding cut until the bleeding stops. This may take one minute or five minutes.
2. Wash your hands so you don't get dirt in your cut.
3. Bandage the cut with the best size bandaid in your kit.
4. If you have a scrape that is bleeding, do your best to wash it well with soap and water. Show it to your mom and dad later to see if it needs another washing so that it won't become infected.
5. Tell your parents how the cut or scrape happened. Ask them to decide if you need a tetanus shot.
6. If you are caring for younger brothers or sisters, be sure to show their wounds to your parents.
7. Write a house rule with your mom or dad so you know whom to call about the cut.

Bad Cuts

1. If blood is gushing or spurting, call 911 or the police. Tell them that you need an ambulance and give them your address and directions to your house.
2. Take a large towel or cloth and hold it tightly against the wound. If you are bleeding from an arm or leg, try to hold it high—above your heart.
3. Just relax and stay calm as you wait for help. Too much movement can make the bleeding worse.

4. Be sure that someone calls your mom or dad as soon as possible.

5. Take a first-aid course so you can learn the pressure points that can be pressed to stop severe bleeding. You can also learn how to tie a special bandage called a tourniquet that also stops severe bleeding.

Nosebleeds

1. Sit with your head up.

2. Pinch your nose closed for at least ten minutes. Do not try to check and see if the bleeding has stopped, until you have pinched your nose for a full ten minutes.

Step 2: How It Can Happen

Everyone else had left the house that morning. Only Vicki, age eleven, was still home, and she was trying to rush her breakfast so she wouldn't be late for school. She picked up a knife to slice her apple, and started to cut. Suddenly, the knife slipped, slicing right into her finger. Blood spurted and Vicki shouted as she jumped back. The cut looked bad. She thought she could see bone.

Vicki grabbed a dishtowel from the sink and wrapped it around her finger. Then she ran next door to the neighbors' house. Their neighbor, Mr. Adams, was on his way to work, but he said he could take her to the hospital emergency room. Since Vicki's family had already given the Adams family five medical release forms to use just in case of an emergency like this, Mr. Adams took one to the hospital.

When they arrived at the hospital, Mr. Adams called Vicki's dad to let him know what had happened. Her father was relieved to know that Mr. Adams had been able to help.

Because it was early in the morning, the doctors at the hospital were able to clean Vicki's cut, neatly sew her wound with five stitches and send her off to school with a large bandage on her finger—before the opening bell rang!

"You were smart to wrap that towel around her finger," said the doctor to Mr. Adams. "Oh, I didn't do that," said Mr. Adams with a proud smile. "Vicki did that herself."

Step 3: Let's Imagine

1. With your parents, make a list of the cuts and bruises emergencies you have had in your family this past year:

2. Now discuss emergencies that have happened to people you know; your friends and relatives. Talk about how they handled the situation and what they might have done.
3. Talk about the danger areas in your house. Do you have extra-sharp knives or sharp edges on counters or furniture?
4. If you have a pet, what would you do if your pet was bleeding or hurt?

   Write that information in your first-aid notebook.

Step 4: Practice

1. Pretend that you have a bad cut. Tell your mom or dad how it happened. Now practice taking care of it yourself, from calling for help to applying pressure.
2. Practice tying large, medium, and small bandages on another person.
3. What if you or a friend started to bleed and you were far away from your first-aid kit? What else can you use to stop bleeding? To make a bandage? List those ideas here:

BURNS: THE FOUR STEPS TO SAFETY

Step 1: What to Do

Minor Burns: Reddened Skin or Blisters

1. Apply ice or very cold water to the burned area. You can do this by running cold water over the burn or soaking the burned area in a bowl of water and ice. If you are burned in an area that you can't soak, apply a cloth pack with ice inside.

2. If your burn covers a large area, you need immediate help. Check with your family so you know whom to call. Be sure this information is in your first-aid notebook.

Serious Burns: White or Charred Skin

1. Call a parent, 911, or the police and tell them you need an ambulance.
2. Do not pull off any clothing or other material that may be stuck to the burn.
3. Do not put *anything* on the burn—no water, no bandage, no ointment.
4. Try to raise the burned area above your heart.
5. Ask someone to reach your parents immediately.
6. Just rest quietly and try to relax until help comes.

Step 2: How It Can Happen

It was the day before Mother's Day and Sylvia, age nine, wanted to do something special for her mom. The family had planned a big party for Sylvia's grandmother, and Sylvia knew her mother was worried about getting the house cleaned up.

As her mom worked and wouldn't be able to clean until later, Sylvia decided to surprise her by finishing all the ironing. She hooked up the iron, filled it with water so it would steam, and reached for a blouse. Her arm hit the iron and knocked it over, and the hot steam water spilled out on her hand.

Sylvia jumped back. Then the iron fell, brushing her leg as it dropped on the floor. While her hand wasn't badly burned, Sylvia's leg had a long red burn mark from the iron.

First, she called her dad to tell him what had happened. He said he would try to get home early to help her, but until then she should do just what the family always did for this kind of burn.

Sylvia immediately filled the kitchen pail with cold water and added a tray of ice. Then she sat in front of the TV while she kept an ice-cold cloth on her leg. Every two minutes or so, she would dip the cloth into the cold pail of water and put it back on her leg. After an hour, the leg looked better and the sting was gone; it never even blistered. Sylvia did get the ironing done! However, she worked slowly and carefully.

Step 3: Let's Imagine

1. With your mom or dad, make a list of the burns you've had in your family this year and what you did for first aid:

2. Discuss the appliances you use in your home that might cause burns, including hair dryers, heaters, even stove tops that get hot when an oven is on. List them here:

3. Write a short story here that tells how you might have a burn emergency in your home or neighborhood. Tell how it happened, what everyone did, and how you got help.

Step 4: Practice

1. With your parents, pretend that you have been badly burned while alone. Practice your immediate reaction to being burned; what you should do first, and how to get help.
2. Practice treating minor burns and serious burns. Use real ice and water. Make an ice pack for an area that is hard to soak.
3. Add several towels to your first-aid kit so you have something to use for ice packs.
4. Think about being burned when water or ice are not available. What can you do in such an emergency? What if you are outside and a friend's clothing catches fire? What can you do? Think about rolling your friend on the ground to put out the fire. What about the burns and all the dirt that may get into the burns? What should you do next? Write your answer here and discuss it with your mom or dad.

BUMPS AND BRUISES

Step 1: What to Do

We all get bumps and bruises. If you have a real lump, make an ice pack and apply it to your lump for an hour while you rest quietly.

If the lump still hurts a lot, call your mom or dad and ask them what you should do next. Tell them how you feel.

If the lump is on your head, tell someone right away if you feel dizzy or confused, have a very bad headache, or start to vomit. Any of these signs mean you must see a doctor immediately. Write these signs in your first-aid notebook.

BITES

Step 1: What to Do

If you are bitten by an animal that belongs to someone else, try to get as much information as you can about the animal—its owner, its size, and color. If you don't know the owner, try to remember the location in the neighborhood where you were bitten. People who live close by may know the animal.

Wash your bite well with soap and water. If it is bleeding, use first aid for bleeding by pressing hard with a clean cloth until the bleeding stops.

Tell your mom or dad right away. You may need to see the doctor and get a tetanus shot.

CHOKING

Step 1: What to Do

The Heimlich Maneuver is especially important to know if you are going to be caring for younger brothers and sisters. This may be simple but it can save a life!

1. Determine if a person is choking; this is likely if the person cannot speak or breathe and begins to turn blue. Little children often choke on food such as cut-up frankfurters or small pieces of candy.

2. Stand behind the victim and wrap your arms around his or her waist as if you were giving him or her a hug. (If the person is sitting, you can kneel and do this, but it is easiest to do standing up.)

3. Make a fist with your thumb extended straight across your tucked fingers. Do not tuck your thumb inside your fingers or try to curl it around your fist.

4. Now place the thumb side of your fist against the victim's abdomen just below the ribs but above the navel.

5. Grab your fist with your other hand and push into the victim's abdomen with quick, upward thrusts. Keep doing this until the victim begins to breathe.

6. If the victim is lying down, kneel across the hips so you are facing the person.

7. Place the heel of one hand on the victim's abdomen, just below the ribs but above the navel; place your other hand on top of the first, and press into the abdomen with quick, upward thrusts.

8. If you find *yourself* choking, lean your abdomen against a table or chair and force your body down so that the furniture will push up and into your abdomen just like someone's fist.

POISON

Step 1: What to Do

1. If you or someone you know is poisoned, call an adult for immediate help. You may need to call 911 or the police.
2. Try to keep the container the poison was in to show the doctors.

ELECTRIC SHOCK

Step 1: What to Do

1. Unplug the appliance that is causing the shock. If you can't do that, try to throw the circuit breaker or remove a fuse. This is why your home emergency practice and notebook is important; you will know just how to do this!
2. If you need to push the victim away without turning off the electricity, *be sure you do not touch the victim or you will be electrocuted, too.* Instead, stand on a dry surface and use a wooden pole to push the person away. Be sure your hands and feet are dry. Be sure there is *no metal* on the wooden pole. You can also use a rope or cloth to pull the person away.
3. Call 911 or the police for help immediately. Even if the victim begins to feel fine, you should see that the person is checked by a doctor.
4. Be sure your mom or dad knows as soon as possible.

FIRST-AID EMERGENCIES: WRITE YOUR OWN "STEPS TO SAFETY"

How They Can Happen

Work with your family to write a short report about each emergency that you have heard about from people you know. For example, do you know someone who choked or had a bad bruise recently? Write what happened here:

Bump or Bruise:

Bite:

Choking:

Poison:

Electrical Shock:

Let's Imagine:

Now look at each emergency and consider how it might happen in your home. Talk this over with your mom or dad and imagine what might happen and how you can respond. Write your ideas here and have your parents read your answers:

Bump or Bruise:

Bite:

Choking:

Poison:

Electrical Shock:

Practice

Take plenty of time here. Practice the correct first-aid actions for:

1. A bump or bruise: both a minor one and what to do if something is serious. What are the signs that the bump or bruise is more serious?

2. A bite: Do you have animals nearby that worry you? Let your parents know that as you practice first aid for bites.

3. Choking: Every family member should practice the "Heimlich Maneuver" on someone standing, sitting, and lying down. You should also practice doing this to yourself.

4. Poison: Practice making a call to the police, telling them how the poisoning happened.

5. Electric shock: Demonstrate the safe way to remove a victim from the electrical power source. Practice removing a fuse or switching off a circuit breaker.

6. Double-check, with your parents, all your emergency phone lists and numbers. Keep extra ones on hand.

7. Practice your first-aid actions regularly. Take a first-aid course if possible.

8. Write all the "What to Do" instructions in your first-aid notebook. This will take some time, but you will really know what to do when you have finished.

SAFETY QUIZ

Take a safety quiz with a friend or with one of your parents. First, each of you write five questions for the different types of emergencies. Ask "What should you do if . . . ?" Write your questions here:

Home Emergencies

1.

2.

3.

4.

5.

Self Emergencies

1.

2.

3.

4.

5.

Neighborhood Emergencies

1.

2.

3.

4.

5.

Now, ask your friend to answer your questions, while you answer your friend's. This is also a good exercise to do with a class. Emergencies can happen to all children, including those who are not in self-care.

10
GETTING INTO COOKING

This chapter has been prepared with the assistance of a professional cook, Judith M. Cooke, whose children have been in self-care for three years.

Mrs. Cooke and her children, Jennifer, age fifteen, and David, age eleven, have experienced the worries all families have when children must spend some time in the kitchen alone. Their recommendations for learning how to cook the safe way have been tested the best way—by kids in self-care!

A GUIDE TO KITCHEN KNOW-HOW

Would you like to be able to come home from school and fix yourself a delicious snack? Would you like to be able to make something special for your lunch box? Would you like to impress and please your whole family by preparing a complete dinner for them some night, all on your own?

This chapter is planned to help you do these things safely and confidently! Some of you may already be familiar with kitchen appliances and cooking techniques. Some of you may be absolute beginners. Whatever your level of expertise, the information here will be of use to you.

This chapter is divided into two parts: a "Cook's Tour Workbook" section and a "Recipe Notebook." Experienced cooks will want to review the basics covered in the Workbook section—use of appliances and equipment, simple techniques of food preparation, and safety rules—before moving on to recipes and complete meal preparation. Beginning cooks, however, should spend special time with adults on the Cook's Tour Workbook section.

As beginners, you should explore each main work area of your kitchen—the stove, oven, and food preparation areas—and write down the answers to the questions we've asked about each of these areas. You should operate appliances, practice techniques, and do the "Cook's Essential Exercises" with your parents, several times. You should make yourself very familiar with the Safety Rules.

After you take the tour and complete the workbook exercises, you should get some "hands-on" confidence-building cooking experiences before you begin to prepare recipes on your own. We suggest you try the confidence-builders we've listed below.

1. *Help an adult prepare a meal.* Start with simple tasks, progress to harder ones.

2. *Offer to be responsible,* on your own, for some meal preparation jobs. For instance: take the meat loaf (that Mom or Dad has fixed the night before) out of the refrigerator at the proper time. Adjust the oven racks, preheat the oven, and put the dish in the oven before Mom or Dad gets home from work.

3. One evening, *you prepare the main dish for dinner;* an adult will prepare the side dishes. The next night, trade responsibilities.

4. Parents often worry about accidents in the kitchen. Be sure to complete the exercises in the "Physical Safety" section so your family knows you are prepared to deal with emergencies such as fire, and to help yourself in case you need first aid for a cut or burn.

First, let's take the "Cook's Tour." We'll begin at the stove work area. As you explore this work area with an adult, be sure to write down the answers to all the questions in the blanks that are provided. In the future, when you are cooking on your own, you will have questions. Maybe no adult will be around to answer them for you. Do you panic? No! If your question is one that is covered in the "Cook's Tour Workbook," you'll have your answer close at hand!

COOK'S TOUR WORKBOOK
STOVE WORK AREA

- Is your stove gas or electric? _____

- Turn on your stove. Turn it to high heat, to medium heat, to low heat. _____

- What should you do if the burner on your gas stove does not light when you turn it on? _____

  Why is it dangerous if the burner does not light? _____

- Where are the pots and pans? _____

- Where are the skillets? What is cooked in these? _____

- Where are the hot pads? What are they used for? _____

- Where do you put a hot pan after you have taken it off the heat? _____

- Where should you put the oil or grease that is sometimes left in a skillet or pan after cooking? _____

Safety Tips

1. Turn handles of pots and skillets to the inside of the stove so that no one will bump into them and knock them off the stove. Also, make sure that the handles are not over another burner. Metal handles get very hot, and plastic ones can melt.

2. Use low or medium heat when cooking fats or oils to avoid spattering.
   If anything begins to smoke, turn off the heat, get a pot holder, and take the pan off the heat. Set the pan on a cold burner.

3. If fat or any substance catches fire in a pan or skillet:
   Turn off heat.
   Cover pan with a lid, or a larger pan, or smother the fire with baking soda.
   Where is the baking soda? _____
   Never use water to extinguish a grease or electrical fire!
   If the fire spreads, leave the house, and telephone the Fire Department from a neighbor's house.

You may have some special notes that you want to make about your stove work area. You may write them in here.

OVEN WORK AREA

- What temperature on your
  oven is high heat? _____
  low heat? _____
  medium heat? _____
- What is broil?
  Why should you keep the oven
  door ajar when you broil? _____
- What pans can you use in the
  oven? _____
  Where are these pans kept? _____
- Take out the oven racks and
  move them to different
  positions. _____
- Turn on the oven. _____
- Turn off the oven. _____

Safety Tips

1. Arrange oven racks *before* you turn on the oven.

2. Always use pot holders when you take something out of the oven.

3. Turn off the oven when the food is removed.

SPECIAL ATTACHMENTS AND MICROWAVE OVENS

Some ovens have *special attachments* such as minute timers, hour timers, delayed start mechanisms, self-cleaning attachments, rotis-series, etc. Ask an adult to discuss these with you and show you how they work. The space below is left blank for you to write in information about these attachments.

The microwave oven is a special sort of appliance. This oven cooks foods very quickly, in about one-third to one-half the time it takes in a regular oven. If you have a microwave oven in your kitchen, you will want to learn from an adult how to operate it. Here are a few things you will want to practice with a microwave oven, and questions you will want to ask about it.

- Turn on the oven.   _____
- Set the timer.   _____
- Stop the timer and open the
  oven door.   _____
- What sort of utensils can you
  use in the microwave oven: _____
  Where are they kept?   _____
- Why should you *not* use metal
  utensils or aluminum foil?   _____
- What can you do in a
  microwave oven that you
  cannot do in a regular oven?   _____

Important Safety Tips for Microwave Ovens

1. Do not operate a microwave oven when it is empty.
2. If the food to be cooked in a microwave is enclosed in a plastic bag, puncture the bag first with a fork before cooking it. Steam builds up in a closed bag, and the trapped steam can cause the bag to explode.

You may have some special notes that you want to make about your oven work area. You may write them in here.

FOOD PREPARATION AREA

There is an area in your kitchen which you will want to set aside as your special place to prepare ingredients *before* you begin to cook them—a place to clean, peel, chop, slice, dice, mix, measure, blend, and process. Following is a list of questions you will want to ask about the tools and appliances used in this area, and operations that you will want to practice with an adult.

Knives

- Where are the knives stored? _____

- Do you have a butcher knife? _____

  What is it used for? _____

  How do you hold it? _____

- Do you have a paring knife? _____

  What is it used for? _____

  How do you hold it? _____

- What is a bread knife? _____

- Where is the cutting board? _____

- How should a knife be
  sharpened? _____

Safety Tips

1. Always keep fingers away from the knife blade.
2. Always use a cutting board when you use a knife; do not cut on the countertop or against your hand. This is for your own safety and also to protect the knife.
3. Wash and dry knives immediately after you use them. Knives should not be left in dishwater to soak. This is bad for the knives, and you might also cut yourself.
4. Be sure to put knives away immediately after you have cleaned them so that a younger child cannot reach them.

Mixers, Blenders

You may have one or all of these appliances in your kitchen. Find out which ones you are allowed to use. Under no circumstances should you operate any of these appliances without adult supervision unless you have specific permission. *Make sure your hands are dry before using any electrical appliance!*
- Where is the electric mixer
  kept? _____

What is it used for?   _____

Where should it be plugged in?   _____
• Fit in the beaters.
• Fit in the mixing bowl.
• *Note:* Do not operate the mixer unless there are ingredients in the
  mixing bowl, as you might damage the machine.

• Where is the blender kept?   _____

  What is it used for?   _____

  Where should it be plugged in? _____
You may have some special notes that you want to make about your
mixer and blender. You may write them here.

Basic Kitchen Tools

You and an adult need to locate these food preparation tools and
practice using them.

                                                Location:

Measuring cups: dry   _____
                 liquid   _____

Measuring spoons   _____

Mixing spoons   _____

Mixing bowls   _____

Vegetable peeler   _____

Potato brush   _____

Strainers and colanders   _____

Cooking fork   _____

Citrus juicer   _____

Rotary beater   _____

Spatulas and pancake turners _____

Rolling pin   _____

Rubber scraper   _____

Kitchen scissors   _____

Tongs   _____

Soup ladles   _____

Graters—fine and coarse   _____

Remember! Cooking is a lot easier and more fun if you wash up as you cook! Nobody likes to finish up a cooking project and have a lot of dirty dishes left in the sink to wash. Also, if you need a certain utensil or pan in the middle of your project, and you find that it is already dirty, you have to stop and wash it. This is inconvenient, and might possibly cause you to ruin whatever it is you are cooking.

Staples

You will also want to find out where these basic ingredients are kept:

flour   _____

sugar   _____

salt and pepper   _____

spices   _____

     _____

oil   _____

vinegar   _____

canned goods   _____

rice   _____

noodles   _____

shortening   _____
    and these supplies:

paper towels   _____

aluminum foil   _____

wax paper   _____

plastic wrap   _____

dish towels   _____

soap   _____

sponges   _____

dishwashing brush   _____

first-aid kit   _____

A COOK'S ESSENTIAL EXERCISES—TO DO WITH AN ADULT

1. *Slice an onion.* Get out the cutting board. Set the onion on the board and, using a sharp knife, cut a flat base on one of the long ends of the onion. Using your fingers, peel off the dry outer skin of the onion. Set the flat base on the cutting board. Now, cut off each end of the onion. Set the onion back on the cutting board on its flat base, and, using a chef's knife, cut the onion into thin slices.

2. *Slice a carrot.* Set the carrot on the cutting board. Use a paring knife to cut off each end of the carrot. Scrape the carrot lengthwise with a vegetable peeler. Discard the peelings. Using a sharp knife, cut the carrot crosswise into thin slices. You will have small "coins" of carrot.

3. *Slice a stalk of celery.* Set the celery on a cutting board. Use a paring knife to cut off the top leafy part of the stalk, and cut off a small slice from the other end of the stalk. Slice the stalk crosswise, so that you will have small, crescent-shaped pieces of celery.

4. *Chop a garlic clove.* Place the clove of garlic on a cutting board. Cut off each end with a sharp paring knife, and remove the dry outer skin. Discard the skin. Then cut the clove with the small knife to obtain six to eight small pieces of the clove.

5. *Chop a green pepper.* On a cutting board, slice off the top and bottom of the green pepper. Cut the pepper in half. Discard the seeds. Using a sharp paring knife, cut out the whitish parts of the inside of the pepper. Cut each half into strips. Arrange the strips lengthwise in a bunch, and cut across the strips to make small dice.

6. *Grate the rind of a lemon,* using a fine grater. *Juice* the lemon.

7. *Grate a soft cheese,* such as cheddar or Swiss, using a coarse grater. Store the cheese in a plastic bag in the refrigerator until you are ready to use it in a recipe.

8. Measure one cup of flour; level it off. Measure 1 tablespoon (T.) of sugar; level it off.

9. Measure one cup of water. Pour it in a sauce pan and bring it to a boil, over high heat.

10. Have an adult show you how to separate the yolk from the white of an egg. Separate two eggs yourself. Put the egg whites in a small bowl, and, using a rotary beater, whip the egg whites until they are stiff.

11. Fry an egg. Measure 1 tablespoon (T.) of butter. Melt it over medi-

um heat in a small skillet. Break an egg into a small bowl. Pour the egg into the skillet. Fry the egg gently. Season it with salt and pepper, and, using a wide spatula, fit it onto a plate. Enjoy!

OK! You've taken the Cook's Tour. You've written down all the answers. You've practiced the Cook's Essential Exercises several times.

Do you and your parents feel comfortable that you know your way around the kitchen? Do you feel that you can handle emergencies?

If the answer is "yes," you're ready to plan some cooking projects. The following section is your "Recipe Notebook." You should write down your family's favorite recipes with the ingredients you like to use. You should also write down the directions your parents think are the safest for your kitchen.

Notice that we are leaving space for you to write a shopping list so that you will have a record of the right ingredients. We are also including a place to record your "count-down time schedule" so you will know just how long it takes to prepare your recipe. Record this time after you have prepared your recipe for the first time.

When you have prepared several recipes on your own, and enjoyed them, you may want to cook a whole meal for your family. Be sure to have permission before you do this.

RECIPE NOTEBOOK

AFTER-SCHOOL SNACKS

List your favorite . . .

Fruits:

Vegetables:

Cookies:

Other favorite snacks and how you make them: (See "Desserts" for some special ideas.)

MAIN COURSES

How does your family like to prepare:
Hamburgers:

Shopping list:

Count-down time schedule:

Frankfurters

Shopping list:

Count-down time schedule:

Spaghetti:

Shopping list:

Count-down time schedule:

Chicken:

Shopping list:

Count-down time schedule:

Meat Loaf:

Shopping list:

Count-down time schedule:

Chili:

Shopping list:

Count-down time schedule:

Macaroni and Cheese:

Shopping list:

Count-down time schedule:

Fish:

Shopping list:

Count-down time schedule:

Favorite Casserole:

Shopping list:

Count-down time schedule:

Tacos:

Shopping list:

Count-down time schedule:

Pizza:

Shopping list:

Count-down time schedule:

Toasted Cheese Sandwiches:

Shopping list:

Count-down time schedule:

TV Dinners:

Shopping list:

Count-down time schedule:

Other family favorites:

SALADS

Tossed Green Salad:

Shopping list:

Count-down time schedule:

Fruit Salad:

Shopping list:

Count-down time schedule:

Coleslaw:

Shopping list:

Count-down time schedule:

VEGETABLES

Fresh vegetables you like:

How to prepare:

Count-down time schedule:

Frozen vegetables you like:

How to prepare:

Count-down time schedule:

Canned vegetables you like:

How to prepare:

Count-down time schedule:

Potatoes:

How to prepare:

Count-down time schedule:

Rice:

How to prepare:

Count-down time schedule:

Now you have written down your family's favorite recipes. Let's think about some special desserts. First, we've left space for your recipes. Then, we've added some of our own that we think you might like to try. They have all been tested—and tasted—by Jennifer and David!

YOUR SPECIAL DESSERTS

(Be sure to include your shopping lists and count-down time schedules!)

OUR SPECIAL DESSERTS

Always ask permission before trying a new recipe. Double-check the ingredients with your mom or dad; they may want you to use certain ones.

SNACKS AND DESSERTS

ORANGE WHIP

1 canned peach half
½ cup orange juice
¼ cup syrup from the peaches

½ cup plain yogurt
¼ tsp. nutmeg
2 ice cubes

Put all ingredients into a blender jar and blend at top speed until mixture is thick and creamy. (1 serving)

EGGNOG

1 egg
1 cup milk
1 T. honey

¼ tsp. vanilla
1 ice cube

Put all ingredients into a blender jar and blend at top speed until mixture is thick and creamy. (1 serving)

APPLE NOG

1 cup apple juice
a small banana

1 egg yolk
2 ice cubes

Put all ingredients into a blender jar and blend at top speed until mixture is thick and creamy. (1 serving)

PINEAPPLE FLIP

1½ cups unsweetened
pineapple juice
1 ripe banana

juice of ½ lemon
2 ice cubes
2 tsp. honey

Put all ingredients into a blender jar and blend at top speed until mixture is thick and creamy. (1 serving)

ENERGY MIX

3 cups mixed nuts and seeds—
sunflower seeds, peanuts,
almonds, cashews, pecans,
walnuts, pepitas—your
choice.

1½ cups black raisins
1½ cups white raisins
1 cup granola cereal

Combine and store in a covered jar or plastic container with a tight-fitting lid. (7 cups)

MUFFIN CHEESE SNACKS

2 T. butter
¼ lb. grated sharp Cheddar
Cheese spread, at room
temperature
1 tsp. Worcestershire sauce
¼ tsp. Tabasco sauce

1 tsp. mustard
2 T. mayonnaise
pinch of garlic salt
pinch of pepper
2 English muffins, split

1. Measure ingredients. Select equipment. Preheat oven to 300 degrees.
2. In a heavy saucepan, combine all the ingredients.
3. Heat over low heat, stirring with a wooden spoon until well-blended and smooth. Remove from heat and let cool a bit.
4. Spread the cheese mixture on the split English muffin halves. Put the muffins on a cookie sheet and bake 8 minutes at 300 degrees. (4 snacks)

BANANA BREAD

1¼ cups flour
1 tsp. baking soda
½ tsp. salt
1 stick butter
1 cup sugar

3 ripe bananas, mashed
together in a small bowl; use a
fork
2 eggs, beaten together in a
small bowl; use a fork
½ cup chopped pecans
(optional)

1. Measure ingredients. Select equipment. Adjust oven racks. Pre-heat oven to 350 degrees.

2. Combine the flour, soda, and salt in a bowl.
3. Put the butter and sugar in the bowl of an electric mixer. Mix together at medium speed until well-blended and creamed.
4. Mix in the mashed bananas and the eggs, using medium speed.
5. Stir in the flour, using a wooden spoon.
6. Stir in the nuts.
7. Pour the batter into a well-greased baking pan. The pan should measure 9" × 5" × 3", approximately. (You will probably need to use a rubber scraper to get all the batter out of the mixing bowl and into the baking pan.)
8. Bake the bread at 350 degrees for 45 to 55 minutes. You can test for doneness this way: Stick a wooden toothpick, or skewer, or knife into the center of the loaf. Pull it out. If it comes out clean (that means with no batter clinging to it), the loaf is done.
9. When the loaf is done, remove it from the oven, using pot holders. Let the loaf cool in the pan about 15 minutes. When the loaf has cooled, set a cooling rack on the counter. Using pot holders, invert the baking pan onto the cooling rack. The bread should fall onto the cooling rack. If it does not, turn the pan over again, and run a table knife around the edges of the loaf. Invert again.
10. When the loaf has fallen onto the rack, turn the loaf right side up and cool completely before cutting into slices. (1 loaf)

JENNIFER'S LEMON BARS

1 cup butter	2 cups sugar
½ cup powdered sugar	4 T. flour
2 cups flour	juice of 2 lemons
¼ tsp. salt	grated rind of 1 lemon
4 eggs	

1. Measure and prepare ingredients. Select equipment. Preheat oven to 325 degrees.
2. Put the butter, powdered sugar, flour (2 cups), and salt into the bowl of an electric mixer. Mix at medium speed until crumbly.
3. Press this mixture evenly into an oblong pan, 9" × 13". Bake 15 minutes at 325 degrees.
4. While this is baking, prepare the lemon topping: mix the eggs, sugar, flour (4 T.), lemon juice and rind, in the mixing bowl of the electric mixer. Mix at medium speed until well blended.

5. When the bottom layer has finished baking, remove the pan from the oven, using pot holders, and set the pan on a trivet on the counter. Pour the topping mixture over the bottom layer, and return the pan to the oven. Bake this for another 25 minutes.
6. Using pot holders, remove the pan from the oven and set it on a trivet on the counter top. Let the bars cool in the pan before cutting them into 24 squares. Sprinkle the bars with more powdered sugar, if you wish. (24 bars)

CHOCOLATE CHIP BARS

1 cup butter	2¼ cup flour
1 cup brown sugar	1 tsp. baking soda
½ cup white sugar	½ tsp. salt
2 eggs	1 12-ounce package of
1½ tsp. vanilla	semisweet chocolate bits

1. Measure and prepare ingredients. Select equipment. Preheat oven to 350 degrees.
2. In the mixing bowl of the electric mixer, combine the butter, brown sugar, and white sugar. Mix at medium speed until the mixture is creamed.
3. Add the eggs and the vanilla, and mix.
4. In a separate bowl, combine the flour, soda, and salt. Add this to the egg-sugar-butter mixture in the mixing bowl. Mix at low speed until combined.
5. Add the water to the batter and mix at low speed until combined.
6. Spread the batter into a buttered 9″ × 13″ baking pan. Spread it out evenly.
7. Bake this 30 minutes at 350 degrees.
8. Using pot holders, remove the pan from the oven, and set the pan on a trivet on the counter top. Let the bars cool. Then cut into 24 squares. (24 bars)

FAMILY CUSTARD

3 eggs	½ tsp. nutmeg
2 cups skim milk	1 T. vanilla
¼ cup sugar	

1. Measure and prepare ingredients. Select equipment. Preheat oven to 350 degrees. Adjust oven rack to middle level.
2. Break eggs into a medium size bowl. Using a rotary beater, beat the eggs until they are well blended.
3. Add the remaining ingredients to the eggs, and beat the mixture with a rotary beater until well blended.
4. Pour the custard into a 1-quart baking dish.
5. Set the baking dish into another shallow baking pan, such as a round or oblong cake pan, and add water to the baking pan. The water should be about 2 inches deep.
6. Put both pans, the custard dish and the pan containing water, into the preheated oven.
7. Bake about 45 minutes. Custard is done when you insert a knife into the center of it, and the knife comes out clean.
8. Let cool on a trivet before serving. (4 to 6 servings)

11

BROTHERS AND SISTERS IN SELF-CARE

HOW WELL DO THEY DO?

Like all self-care situations, each family's experience reflects the individuality of the children and the parents. Some families succeed at having brothers and sisters together in self-care while others do not. Success appears to be the result of many factors, including parents' willingness to discuss and plan self-care *with their children.*

Many parents and children have shared their self-care experiences with us. It is remarkable how many children tell of using sophisticated parenting skills in caring for brothers and sisters. These children often feel proud of how well they care for younger brothers and sisters. Yet others report being physically hurt by an older brother or sister who may have reached the end of sibling patience. Not surprisingly, these children dislike being cared for by a brother or sister.

However, in almost all families where there are just two children, when each child has been given the choice to be home alone or with a brother or sister, most have preferred to be in self-care with the brother or sister! Positive remarks by many children show that brothers and sisters at home together in self-care often form close attachments. "My sister helps me with my homework," said one child. "I am not so lonely when my brother is home," said another. "When I get scared, I go to my big sister," said a nine-year-old boy.

The self-care experience is as different for the child who is the oldest as it is for the younger child. Many "oldests" enjoy caring for brothers and sisters. They enjoy having company after school.

Yet some "oldests" speak of feeling angry "at having to care for them" or "at having younger children tag along." They feel frustrated because "they never listen to me" or "never do what I say." They feel sad "because I never have any time to myself."

Younger children have their complaints, too. A questionnaire given to younger children elicited many complaints of mistreatment by older children: "My older brother yells at me," "he hits me," "she beats me," "he won't let me watch television," "I can't have snacks." Many reported the older child "just ignores me."

To reduce this kind of conflict will be one goal of a good self-care plan.

HOW TO DESIGN BROTHER AND SISTER SELF-CARE PLANS

Before establishing house rules and other activities for your children, consider these two alternatives for organizing self-care responsibilities:

1. Child in Charge

Many parents elect to place one child in charge of the other children in the family. This child, usually the oldest, is responsible for watching younger children, responding to emergencies, enforcing rules, and reporting problems to parents. Parents often find this plan successful when the responsible child is at least three to four years older than the other children.

The mother of a twelve-year-old girl and two boys, ages six and seven, said of the use of the "child in charge" plan with her children, "My daughter watches my two sons after school from three to five o'clock. She walks home with the boys from school, fixes snacks, and supervises as they watch television or play games. If one of the boys breaks a house rule, she is instructed to call me and to send her brother to his room. Twice a week a teen-age baby-sitter watches the boys while my daughter attends band practice."

2. In Charge of Self

In self-care situations where children are close in age or are able to care for themselves, parents often prefer that each child be responsible for his or her own care. The children are expected to follow house rules, perform separate chores, and report problems to parents. When problems occur, the parents resolve them with the individual child or they help mediate difficulties between the children.

The mother of two girls, ages thirteen and fifteen, described her use of the "in charge of self" plan: "As the girls fought constantly when my oldest daughter was in charge, we now have each girl responsible for herself. Both girls are allowed to visit friends and to have a friend visit once a week. Each has her own rules and list of chores. In fact, I assign them chores in separate rooms and rotate the chores weekly. When there are problems, we sit down together and try to work them out."

Both of the above methods can help you succeed in assigning self-care responsibilities. Before actually designing your family's self-care plan, we want you to consider the following factors that may affect your children's behavior.

PROBLEMS BETWEEN BROTHERS AND SISTERS

"A Fight a Day . . ."

Fighting is the most common problem reported by children in self-care. Parents reinforce that fact. As one parent said, "Last week it was a picture my son broke when he threw a ball at his sister. This week I had three phone calls about whose turn it was or wasn't to watch TV! Most nights I'm almost afraid to go home for fear someone has been hurt."

Children report the same worries. In self-care it is not unusual that fights occur daily between the children in the family. "He yells at me," "she doesn't give me my turn," "he hits me"—all are common complaints.

Why do children fight in self-care? For the same reasons they fight when parents are home. One common response is that the children enjoy fighting. Some feel it's even more fun if you can get a brother or sister in trouble. Children also respond that fighting is "something to do." Some find it a good way to get attention from Mom and Dad. In self-care, younger children may fight when bossed by older brothers or sisters, while the older children are trying to control the behavior of their younger family members.

Things do get better, but they get better slowly. Studies show that it's possible to look at children's ages and predict how much they will fight with a brother or sister. For example, the most stressful relationships occur between children who are close in age, generally within one to three years.

Also, children ages six, eight, ten and eleven tend to get along poorly with both older and younger siblings with one exception; ten-year-olds are somewhat successful with older siblings. Fortunately, seven- and nine-year-olds are more pleasant in their relationships with brothers and sisters as well as with other people.

From age twelve and up, relationships—particularly with siblings four or more years *younger*—definitely improve. By age fifteen, most children have learned to walk away from fights with younger siblings, and report even better relationships with older siblings. By age sixteen, most young teens are more concerned with relationships with their peers and have little interest in continued fights with brothers or sisters.

Thus, age twelve can be a guideline for deciding whether or not your child is ready for the responsibility for younger siblings in self-care. However, as this chapter indicates, many other factors must be considered.

Fighting is a common practice for children, whether they are in self-care or are supervised. Children in self-care, however, are sometimes more alarmed by the fighting because there is no parent close by to help if the fight gets out of hand.

Reducing Conflict in Self-Care

While some fighting is normal and is to be expected in self-care, it is possible to structure your self-care situation in ways that can reduce conflict. Consider these suggestions:

1. Separate your children as much as possible. Consider alternate days for children to participate in school activities, visiting

friends, bringing friends home (they can go to separate rooms to play), or going to stay with a relative or neighbor.

2. Avoid situations that will lead to conflict such as doing the same chores together, playing games that always seem to end with fighting, or having friends over who help start fights.

3. Enforce "no hitting" rules when you are home. Any time one child hits another, disciplinary steps should be taken.

4. Provide ways that children can release pent-up energy and emotion. Physical activity after school, or when you return home, is a constructive way to relieve frustration.

5. Plan for time at home when you can give each of your children positive attention. Praise all your children together when they have good days in self-care.

6. Be alert to problem areas for children in self-care together. Parents have learned that children frequently fight over TV shows, snacks, and who should do which chore. Anticipate these conflicts in your household, and provide solutions before they occur. Make up a weekly television schedule, provide snacks that may be different for each child, and vary the list of daily chores.

When to Intervene in Fights

The quandary faced by all parents is *when and how to intervene in children's fights*. To help decide, ask yourself the following questions each time one of your children complains about a problem with a brother or sister:

1. Is this normal bickering or a more serious problem that needs my attention? Is this a complaint that can be ignored? ("She took my hat!") Or is this a matter that demands immediate attention? ("He hit me with the yardstick!")

2. Have I heard this problem before? If a child repeatedly says, "I didn't get to watch TV," then it is clear that the child can't resolve the problem and you need to intervene.

3. Is my child really upset? If so, the least you must offer your child is support for finding a solution to the problem. You may need to do more.

Ideally, children can solve their own problems, but many have not yet reached a point of maturity with adequate problem-solving skills. When your children report a problem to you that you feel needs resolution, the following steps may be helpful:

1. Ask each child to tell his or her side of the story.
2. Discuss the problem and how each child tried to solve it.
3. Brainstorm solutions together and help your children decide on one that is agreeable to everyone.
4. Remain neutral throughout the discussion. Do not side with one child. Do not make one feel at fault.

Some children do not discuss problems well, or they may feel intimidated by older brothers and sisters. If one or more of your children seems to have difficulty expressing his or her feelings and ideas, ask the child to write down answers to these questions:

---

1. What do I think the problem is?

2. How have I tried to solve it?

3. Write three possible solutions:

Problem-Solving by Phone

Brothers and sisters in self-care often call parents at work for help in solving self-care problems. This is difficult to do in a short time, having heard only one side of the problem. Unless an immediate response is necessary, a parent should ask the child how the problem might be solved for the moment until the parent gets home. Support the child in the decision and continue the discussion when you arrive home.

If the children appear to be out of control, take time to let everyone cool off. Recommend an activity that will separate the children—"John, you watch television and, Tommy, you go over to Mike's house." This will ease the situation until you can get home.

Phone calls in which you are asked to solve such problems can be avoided by establishing a regular time at home for discussing problems. Then, if you are called with a problem, you can simply remind the child that it can be discussed at the appropriate time.

MORE SERIOUS PROBLEMS BETWEEN
BROTHERS AND SISTERS

Physical and Verbal Abuse

Children in the care of brothers and sisters occasionally report physical and verbal abuse. Such abusive situations can result in severe physical and emotional damage to children.

"When they won't listen, I get my father's gun out," one child in charge of brothers and sisters told us. "That really scares them."

More often, children tell of using boards and other objects in their attempts to discipline younger children; sometimes out of frustration, sometimes with malicious intent.

While it can be difficult to distinguish abusive acts from normal fighting, the following signs can help you judge if abuse is occurring:

1. Physical injury that is not consistent with the explanation given by the child.
2. A younger child's fear of an older sibling.

Sexual Abuse

Younger children in self-care will sometimes report sexual abuse by older children in the family. Although such reports are not common, all parents should be aware of the potential for sexual abuse.

It can occur between children regardless of their sex—brother can molest brother, sister can molest sister. To know the symptoms and the proper action to take if you have reason to believe that sexual abuse may be a problem for your children, read

Chapter Seven, "Your Neighborhood"—the section on "Physical Safety."

If you think that one of your children is being molested by an older brother or sister, question the child who may be the victim. Be direct; ask if a brother or sister is touching parts of the child's body that shouldn't be touched. "Telling on" a brother or sister is difficult unless a child is directly asked.

If your child confirms your fear, seek professional help immediately. Remember, sexual molestation is not *normal* sexual curiosity; it is a signal that professional help is needed.

DO'S FOR BROTHER/SISTER CARE

As you begin to design a self-care plan that will involve more than one child, we recommend that you keep these points in mind:

1. Be clear about which responsibilities are to be handled by each child, and which are to be managed by a parent.

2. Teach *each* child how to respond to emergencies. Too often, only the oldest child knows, leaving younger children unable to care for themselves if the oldest child is not available.

3. Allow time, whenever possible, for each child to pursue individual interests.

4. Keep the self-care hours short. The child in charge needs time off from stressful day-care responsibilities. Each child needs time away from brothers and sisters.

Now you are ready to design your family's self-care plan. Carefully consider the following section.

HOW TO MANAGE BROTHERS AND SISTERS

All children who supervise other children should understand appropriate ways to respond when there are problems. The right response can help a child avoid misbehaving.

These responses can be invaluable for the child in charge. Work with your oldest child to be sure each of these is fully understood. Write in responses that are particularly appropriate for your household.

1. Empathize! Try to understand how your younger brother or sister is feeling. Is he or she tired? Bored? Lonely? Once you can understand *why* something is happening, you will be better able to correct the problem.

Do you have brothers or sisters who tend to tire easily? Do they get lonely or bored? What helps them feel better? Ask your mom or dad for suggestions. Write a few suggestions here:

2. Praise good behavior. Perhaps all your young sibling needs is good, positive attention. Learn to give praise for the smallest things done well; your brother or sister will love you for it!

List here some of the good things that the younger children in your family are likely to do:

3. Divert a troublesome child's attention with constructive activity such as reading or playing a game. List some family favorites here:

4. Plan separate activities for children who are fighting. List here some ways to separate different children in your family:

5. Trade privileges when two children want the same thing. What privileges can be traded? List here some special trades that you might encourage brothers and sisters to make:

6. Put away those things that the children fight over most often. List them here:

HOW TO DESIGN THE "CHILD-IN-CHARGE" PLAN

If you have decided that the best way to organize your self-care situation is to have one child supervise younger brothers and sisters, work with your children to carefully outline the responsibilities of the child in charge.

Being responsible for the care of younger children is a difficult task. When a child supervises others, he or she is acting as a substitute parent—a job that requires many complex skills. The responsibilities and the ways to carry out those responsibilities need to be clearly understood by the child in charge and by all the other children. Be sure to list all these responsibilities as part of your family's self-care contract, after they have been fully discussed by those family members involved in self-care.

Responsibilities of the Child in Charge

Begin by detailing the exact responsibilities of the child in charge:

- Should he or she be responsible for solving problems and enforcing rules?

  If so, which house rules require enforcement. Be sure to list them.

- Should he or she remind the other children of house rules and report all misbehavior to parents?

- Should he or she call a parent each time there is a problem? What about matters involving physical safety? Whom should the child call first?

Experiment with different ways of assigning responsibility. Children in charge often complain that unless they are able to discipline children when they misbehave, younger children do not listen to what they say. At the same time, older children who are given a great deal of authority in enforcing rules sometimes abuse those privileges and neglect the rights of the younger children.

In most situations, it is best for parents to enforce rules and follow up violations with disciplinary consequences. However, at times the child in charge may have to enforce rules, particularly if one or more children are out of control and safety is the issue.

If the child in charge is to have the authority to enforce rules, clearly specify those rules and the consequences of not following them. For example, if a younger child is not to leave the yard but breaks the rule, should the child in charge call a parent? Should the younger child be brought home and made to spend "time out" in a particular chair?

Responsibilities of the Younger Children

The responsibilities of the younger children also need to be defined. These children should fully understand that they are responsible for their own behavior. They should also understand the consequences of not following rules.

Often, a child in charge is not able to enforce rules with younger children. If this occurs, he or she should not be punished because the younger children did not behave.

Responsibilities of the Parents

The responsibilities of the parents need to be outlined. Parents should discuss the day's problems with the children each night—what happened, and how it was managed. These discussions can help the child in charge learn how to supervise younger children, while all the children can learn ways to manage conflict. This is also the time that disciplinary measures should be taken.

Finally, the child in charge is a substitute parent. Some younger brothers and sisters may feel close to the older child and may continue to relate to that child as a parent even when the parents are home. Older children may like these feelings of power and admiration and may not give them up easily. It is important that parents assertively remind children they are home and in charge again.

Discipline

Clearly define what the disciplinary measures will be. Please note that a very helpful technique for children to use is to designate "time out" in a certain chair or room for a specific time limit.

It is best to help the child in charge plan for disciplinary measures that do not involve hitting or spanking another child. Such a response may worsen the conflict, do nothing to resolve the problem, and result in physical harm to a child.

List all the agreed-upon measures in your family self-care contract.

HOW TO DESIGN A "SELF-IN-CHARGE" PLAN

"Self-in-charge" assumes that each child is responsible for his or her own care and will follow the basic self-care family agreements discussed in Chapter Fifteen, "How to Design Your Self-Care Plan." However, you will want to add some rules that govern how the children will or will not interact in the house when you are not there.

For example, Janet and Susan are each responsible for their own behavior. However, we have these rules for:

---

1. Emergencies that occur when both are home—who is responsible for calling parents, administering first aid, taking charge of home emergencies?

2. Ways to resolve potential fights without calling Mom or Dad:

3. Other:

EVALUATING BROTHER/SISTER SELF-CARE

How can a parent tell when brothers and sisters are getting along well in self-care? How does a parent determine when fighting is serious enough to cause emotional harm?

You can evaluate your family's self-care plan by answering these questions:

1. Do my children spend time together in positive ways: playing, enjoying, and helping one another?
2. Is the fighting worse since we started our self-care plan?
3. Is the arguing and fighting really ugly? Do scratches or bruises indicate physical abuse or too much hitting?
4. How many of my children are complaining about being home with brothers and sisters?
5. Am I worried that something serious will happen to the children while I am away?

If the answers to these questions suggest that your family does have problems with self-care, talk with each child separately. Ask each child to be honest with you. How does he or she feel about being home with brothers or sisters? What are the major problems? Does the child worry that something terrible may happen? (Remember our suggestion of a written questionnaire for children who have difficulty discussing these problems.)

Besides talking with your children, continue to watch and listen. Children in self-care are often reluctant to tattle on one another. Call home each day to check on how things are going. Ask to speak to a different child as older children sometimes leave younger ones alone when they are supposed to be in charge. Ask a neighbor or relative to visit occasionally. While this is a good way to check on your household, it can also be a nice break for the children.

If you feel that the self-care plan is not working, consider these alternatives:

1. Separate the children more frequently.
2. Place one or all of your children in supervised care.
3. Consider family counseling to improve the relationships between your children.

Special Note: You may list here some responses that should also be written into your family's self-care plan. Please check so that important points are not forgotten.

12
THE YOUNG TEEN

As children leave elementary school to attend junior high or middle school, they also enter adolescence—the exciting, mystifying world of teendom.

For many parents, the emergence of the young teen means that a child has new and different needs for supervision. Some parents feel more secure and see their child as ready to assume more responsibility, ready to handle more problem-solving. Other parents feel quite the opposite. Reports of young teens in trouble with sex, alcohol, drugs, and vandalism leave many parents anxious about their child's ability to manage new freedoms in a safe and wise manner.

"When my son was in fifth and sixth grades, everything was o.k.," said one mother. "He stayed home, obeyed our rules and was very dependable. When he started junior high, I decided to quit my full-time job and work at home. The change in him was really something! He simply refused to follow rules and he spent a lot more time with friends."

It's clear that designing self-care plans for young teens requires a great deal of thought, preparation, and experimentation. Each new entrant into the complex world of adolescence has different needs and those needs may change from one day to the next. In order to design a self-care plan for a young teen, parents need to understand the developmental tasks of this age period.

EARLY ADOLESCENCE—A STRESSFUL TIME

Early adolescence, the years between twelve and sixteen, is one of the most stressful times for the young teen and the family. This period has been described as one in which a child reshapes his or her personality—from childhood to adolescence to adulthood. During adolescence, the young teen is expected to form an identity, become less dependent on parents, and learn to establish meaningful relationships with peers and other adults.

At the same time, the young teen is learning to think in more abstract ways, broadening the concrete understandings of childhood. Also, the body changes in ways alternately pleasing and alarming. No wonder the behavior of the young teen may be unpredictable—one moment mature, another moment as impulsive as a five-year-old.

Few parents escape the frustration voiced by a mother who told us, "Most of the time Jamie is so responsible and then, for reasons I can never understand, he turns into one of the most childish fourteen-year-olds . . . I just worry."

While the internal personality changes are stressful, so are the pressures of the environment that the young teen is now experiencing. Each is trying to find his or her way through a new and complex school system. At the same time, the young teen is beginning to test new skills in forming friendships with others, both male and female. Conflict at home often increases as the young teen wants to make more decisions in all these areas while being more influenced by peers and other adults.

SELF-CARE PLANS FOR YOUNG TEENS

Any successful self-care plan for a child will be based on the physical and emotional needs of the individual child; this is definitely true for the adolescent!

Experts have identified several characteristic needs of the young teen that provide clues to the activities and experiences that will make a self-care plan workable:

A Need for Clearly Defined Limits

In any situation the young teen needs to be very well informed of parental rules or limits. Since an adolescent often feels much of the world is uncertain, the structure of good self-care can provide for feelings of safety and security. Unclear rules will mean that the child is more likely to have difficulty following through with correct behavior or responsibilities. House rules, for example, should be established or reestablished on an ongoing basis so the young teen is kept aware while being included in the decisions.

A Need for Positive Experiences with Other People

Relationships with peers and other adults have a special significance during these years. While the parent-child relationship is important, the other friendships help prepare the young teen for an independent adulthood. When possible, find ways for your child to spend time with others, whether just "messing around" or in organized activity.

A Need for Self-Discovery

These young people are eager to learn about themselves and how they fit into the world. Many devour magazines, listen for hours to the radio, and scan the newspaper headlines for news of their favorite rock stars or sports heroes. They look for activities that help define, identify, and broaden their relationships and experiences beyond the family.

Encourage your teen to become a part of your community by taking trips to local libraries and gathering spots as well as places of special interest such as historical sites, the zoo, or an art gallery. Also encourage contact with many different kinds of people—little kids who need baby-sitting, older people who may need some special looking after, men and women involved in unusual careers or hobbies, community organizations that may need assistance. The more the young teen can do successfully on his or her own, the more the parent will see evidence of an emerging maturity.

A Need for Variety

Recognize that at this age, interests change quickly; sometimes overnight. What is terrific today is boring tomorrow. Familiarity with the varied programs available in your community can help fill the young teen's schedule with music and art lessons, dance classes, and sports; even organized jaunts to the shopping center.

A Need for Physical Exercise

Few teens are lacking in an abundance of sheer physical energy. Each may require a different level of activity, but all young teens need the opportunity to release their energies through physical activities such as sports, or dance, or even theatre. Know what your community offers in its recreation programs, theatre groups for young teens, and other organizations including churches, local YMCAs and YWCAs. Today, some organizations have developed after-school programs that are specially designed for the young teen in self-care.

A Need for Autonomy

Teens need room to make mistakes. Testing judgment is an important stage in adolescent development. Too often, parents are overprotective of girls, fearing for their safety. They tend to limit girls' opportunities to engage in sports, see friends, and leave the house while in self-care. However, no data show that girls are in greater danger than boys. Also, girls tend to be given more responsibility for the care of younger children. This can seriously affect their autonomy in self-care.

A Need to Feel Good About Oneself

This is a critical time for experiencing a sense of reward and accomplishment. Encourage activities that help the young teen feel good about himself or herself—academic interests, special talents, athletic skills, music lessons, or volunteer efforts. Too often our children are placed in highly competitive activities, which leave them feeling as though they have failed. Help your young teen find that special niche in an activity in which he or she is valued.

ONE FAMILY'S YOUNG TEEN SELF-CARE PLAN

Sue is twelve years old. She and her parents worked together to plan her self-care situation.

"First of all," said her father, "we want a flexible schedule. We try to designate certain days for different activities, but let Sue decide which activities or friends will be scheduled. For example, we agreed that two days a week she would be involved in organized activity such as classes or team sports. Sue then selected the sport or class."

> ### Sue's Current Schedule
>
> Monday—"Messing around" at home.
>
> Tuesday—Basketball practice or game.
>
> Wednesday—Visit or shop with a friend.
>
> Thursday—Basketball practice or game.
>
> Friday—Chores and relaxation.

"I like the change," said Sue. "Really, I don't get bored."

"We're happy," added her mother. "We work hard to balance the schedule because we feel it's important that she have time with friends, time alone, time in organized activities, and time for physical exercise."

Currently, Sue's parents are very actively involved in her planning. By the time she turns fifteen, however, she may want to make more of the decisions herself. The older the teen, the more the parents' power is effectively exercised through influence and encouragement rather than through direct involvement.

YOUR YOUNG TEEN SELF-CARE PLAN

Not all self-care plans can be as flexible as Sue's. Some parents and teens face difficulties with transportation, lack of good programs in their communities, neighborhoods that are not safe, or responsibility for younger brothers and sisters.

What can a family do when the flexibility of a self-care plan is very limited?

Consider the following:

1. Keep the self-care hours short. Don't assume that since a child is older, he or she is able to manage more than two to three hours a day.

2. Explore all the social and entertainment opportunities in the home. What reading materials are available? Note that reading

is the second favorite pastime of children in self-care. Encourage phone time with friends. Young teens enjoy spending an incredible amount of time on the telephone. What kind of physical activity can a child do at home? Soccer in the backyard?

3. What kinds of trades can you work out with friends, neighbors, and other parents? Could someone take care of a younger child so your teenager is free for an activity once a week? Could you offer weekend baby-sitting in return for transportation to a special event?

4. Enhance evening activities in order to balance the time spent alone after school—allow friends to visit or spend the night, encourage participation in a church youth group, an evening at the library, or the movies.

SELF-CARE ACTIVITY CHART FOR TEENAGERS

Encourage your young teen to complete this chart, or use it as a guideline for discussions. It may be the first time you will become aware of the full range of interests your child has as an adolescent. You can then use it for planning self-care now and in the future.

Things I Would Most Like to Do Right Now

Classes:

Hobbies:

Theatre and dance activities:

Team sports (basketball, soccer, volleyball, swim team):

Individual sports (running, gymnastics, working out):

Musical instruments:

Pastimes (shopping, movies, visiting):

Volunteer or paid work (help with church group, baby-sit):

Places I'd like to go (famous, historical, day-trip, exploring, hiking, other):

People I'd like to see (younger, my age, older, friends, relatives, neighbors):

Some special things I'd really love to do some day (such as learn to ride a horse, play the drums or the saxophone, build an excellent record collection, walk across the North Pole). Even if it seems outrageous, write it down because you never know.

Look at this chart again in four to six months. You may surprise yourself and want to make a lot of changes, or no changes!

FREEDOM—WHAT IS REASONABLE?

One of the major developmental tasks of adolescence is renegotiating the parent-child relationship in a way that enhances the child's ability to move from being dependent on parents to being self-sufficient. This is a difficult task; one that often seems even more difficult for families where the parents are not home to manage mistakes and problems as they occur.

To assume that a young teen needs autonomy in making decisions is not to assume that he or she does not need structure. The question is: what rules or structure should a parent enforce?

Each young teen lives in a family and experiences the kinds of responsibilities that are part of living with others. Sometimes these are not always clear to parents: young teens are accustomed to informing their families that "none of my friends have to follow such stupid rules." Well, be assured that the following rules are ones followed by many parents of young teens.

COMMON HOUSE RULES

1. Before leaving the house, tell us where you will be and when you will be home.

    Some parents require a day's notice or even a week's notice if transportation will be needed. Others require a phone call before the child leaves the house or a note that includes all details of where a child has gone. Parents have the right to declare certain places—judged by them to be inappropriate for their child—off-limits.

2. Complete house chores.

    Young teens live in the home and should be responsible for helping with its upkeep.

3. Be home on time. If you will be late, call.

    Being late and failing to make a phone call is often handled with a loss of privileges or being grounded.

4. Let me know whom you are going to have in the house.

Having friends over when parents are not home is something that should be acknowledged and approved of by parents. Friends who do not act responsibly should not be invited back.

Special note: Young teens need more social contact than younger children. They should be able to have friends over more often and to visit friends in their homes. This is an area where they definitely need more autonomy.

DECISION-MAKING

While clear expectations are necessary for success with young teens in self-care, so is the need for them to make some of their own decisions. At this age, they should be allowed to choose the activities—assuming such activities are safe and constructive—in which they wish to participate. In fact, few are willing to do anything if it is parent-directed.

Young teens should also be able to select their own friends. If they have friends who parents feel are not responsible, then parents can refuse to have these friends in the house when they are not home.

Young teens should have the right to structure most of their free time. One of the advantages for a child in self-care is learning to use free time constructively. This skill allows the young teen even more autonomy in setting the rules that govern the family's self-care plan. It is a skill learned only by practice.

Basically, the older the child, the more he or she should participate in development of the family agreements.

THE FAMILY CALENDAR

One hazard of life with young teens is their short attention span and impulsive behavior; they want to be free to go at any moment, and often make plans just moments before they go. This is behavior guaranteed to be hard on parents!

One mother we interviewed tried to build flexibility into the family schedules by designing a weekly calendar. Every Sunday evening the calendar was posted on the kitchen wall. The two teens in the household, boys ages fifteen and thirteen, then wrote down their school activities, sports events, and any other plans that they already knew about.

Any activity requiring transportation had to be written down two days ahead. All other activities could be written down the night before. If activities were not listed, and scheduling conflicts arose, the boys had to cancel their plans or get their own transportation. After they had missed a few events, the boys took the calendar seriously and it continues to work well for the household.

WRITING THE FAMILY CONTRACT

In Chapter Fifteen, "How to Design Your Self-Care Plan," a family contract with a comprehensive list of self-care rules and agreements is fully described. After reading that chapter, complete a family contract with your young teen. You may want to adapt your contract for your young teen by loosening the rules for friends:

- Friends — who may be in the home?
- Places where you may go:
- Places where you may not go:
- How will you tell us where you are? How much notice must you give? What other specifics do we need to know from you? Will you be in a car with someone?

Keep in mind that young teens are very likely to resist self-care rules. An occasional breach can be expected as they often choose to take consequences rather than comply with rules. If too many rules are being broken too often, consider the following:

1. The rules may not allow for enough decision-making by your young teen.
2. Your child may not like self-care.
3. You may need to provide more supervision.

HOW TO DISCUSS SELF-CARE PROBLEMS

When problems occur that are related to self-care, any talk about these can turn into angry, resentful confrontations between parent and young teen. Remember that adolescence is a time of self-doubt, when the slightest criticism can be viewed as an attack by a parent. Thus, sensitivity is the key to good discussions of problems.

The following guidelines can be helpful:

1. Carefully choose the time to talk the problems over with your child. Talking about it when he or she is still upset is not a good time as most young teens are already angry with themselves when they have made a mistake or slipped up on responsibilities; defenses are up!

2. Keep the discussion short. Lectures get tuned out.

3. Focus on constructive action that can be taken in the situation: "How can we handle this problem?" Criticism will not help.

4. Enforce consequences when appropriate. However, first review why the incident occurred. Was it the result of a misunderstanding? Inappropriate rules? Insufficient skills? Work *with* your young teen to correct the situation.

ALCOHOL, DRUGS, AND SEX

Parents who are considering self-care for young teens often express concern that their children may experiment with alcohol, drugs, or sex if left unsupervised. These concerns are realistic, particularly if you consider the following statistics:

- Older teenagers who are heavy drinkers report taking their first drink before the age of twelve.
- Among eighth graders, average age thirteen, twenty to thirty percent drink excessively.
- Girls under age fifteen are the only group of women in this country for whom the birth rate is not declining.
- The average age for beginning sexual activity is between ages fifteen and sixteen.

Whether children who are home alone are more vulnerable to these problems, we do not know. We do know, however, that parents need to take as many precautions as possible.

Alcohol and Drugs

What can a parent do to prevent drinking problems? These suggestions can be helpful for teenagers who will be home alone:

1. Take the time to teach your child about the effects of alcohol and drug abuse. Work with your adolescent to help them learn ways to say "No." Acknowledge that peer pressure is persuasive.

2. Provide a good example with your own behavior. It is tough to tell a teenager about the evils of alcohol and drugs if you are misusing them.

3. Lock up alcohol and drugs in your home. Keep track of alcohol left in the refrigerator. Teenagers often report watering down alcohol or sneaking beers when parents are not at home. Secret drinking seems exciting, dangerous; don't take chances with your children.

4. Listen and watch. Teenagers often tell brothers and sisters or friends what is really going on. Watch for changes in behavior that might signal drug or alcohol problems. Check with the National Council on Alcoholism and local drug rehabilitation programs in order to recognize warning signals.

Teen Sex

Over the last ten years, sexual activity among teenagers has increased while the age of first sexual encounters has dropped. In the 1970s, the average age for a first sexual experience was between ages eighteen and nineteen; now it is between ages fifteen and sixteen!

While most parents express concern over teenage sexual activity, those whose children are often home alone worry about the unsupervised time. Consider the following as you prepare for self-care and want to safeguard your young teen's emergence into sexual maturity:

1. Take time to discuss sex with your young teen. Most adolescents are eager to learn all they can about sex. Discuss sexual values as well as information.

If your child seems embarrassed to talk with you, look for good reading materials; but read them first yourself. You can select those points or issues that you feel may present some questions. Check with your child after he or she has also read the material, and ask for his or her opinion on those particular points.

2. Prohibit or limit visits from friends of the opposite sex when parents are not home. Enlist a neighbor's support if you suspect that rules are being broken.

3. Select appropriate television programs when you are home with your child. Many programs today not only show sexually stimulating material but actively encourage young people to engage in sexual activity. Approving such programs in your home sends mixed messages to your teenager about your own standards and values.

13

SUMMER CARE

This chapter is written for parents of children ages twelve and over. Few children younger than age twelve have the maturity to be home alone in self-care during the summer.

Of all the child-care problems faced by parents and children, summer care presents the most difficult challenge. The long hours, combined with few places to go, lack of transportation, and little to do, leave parents and children frustrated with summer plans. Even when parents make arrangements for supervised care, the alternatives are seldom satisfactory. Day-care centers are generally designed for children under ten, while children who are age ten or above are often not pleased with the summer day-care that is available.

"I would send my child to any good summer program," complained one mother, "but I can't find one that my thirteen-year-old son will go to."

As a result, many parents feel that the only alternative for their child is being home alone in the summer time.

IS YOUR CHILD READY FOR SUMMER CARE RESPONSIBILITIES?

The answer to this question is not an easy "yes" or "no." As with all self-care questions, the answer is, in part, dependent on your child's abilities, the environment, and the design of the self-care plan.

In reviewing your child's abilities, the best indicator of how well prepared a child is for summer self-care is past performance.

149

For example, how well has your child cared for himself or herself for shorter periods of time, before and after school?

If your child has demonstrated well-developed skills and abilities in self-care, if your parent/child relationship is good, and if your neighborhood is safe and supportive, your child may be ready for summer self-care. On the other hand, if past self-care situations have not been successful, reconsider leaving your child alone. Instead, plan ways to improve in problem areas.

HOW TO DESIGN YOUR CHILD'S
SUMMER SELF-CARE PLAN

Although you may have decided that your child is prepared for self-care, this is only the first step. Now comes careful planning for daily self-care experiences. Summer self-care plans require particular and continual attention from parents as summer hours are long and each self-care plan must be tailored to the individual needs of each child.

Summer self-care plans should be responsive to the basic needs that all children have to develop in a healthy, normal environment. These needs include: safety, peer support, physical activity, stability, and responsibility. Such needs cannot be met when children are home alone eight to ten hours without positive interaction with other children or adults.

In planning for summer self-care, begin by listing, with your child, all activities that will be offered for children in your community this summer. Review Chapter 12, "The Young Teen," and have your child complete the lists of special interests and activities.

Consider programs offered by churches and camps, look at educational and outdoor activities. Can you schedule visits with relatives?

Make another list of all the places where you and your child feel he or she can safely go for recreation and entertainment. These may include:

parks	libraries
recreation centers	shopping centers
school playgrounds	swimming pools
friends' homes	

Finally, list all the people who may be able to help your children in summer care. Consider the following:

neighbors   friends' parents
hired sitters   adult friends
relatives

In arranging summer plans together, remember that the most important ingredient is stability in the form of a structured routine that is varied but predictable.

Each spring, for example, Martha and Steve, parents of a fifteen-year-old daughter and a twelve-year-old son, map out—with help from their children—summer care plans.

The summer is planned so that weekly activities include time at home in self-care as well as time in more structured experiences.

"We have the children stay at home together one week at the beginning of the summer, one week in the middle, and one week before school starts. The rest of the summer is divided between camps, day school (for the younger child), time with relatives, and our family vacations," said Steve.

He and Martha are careful to plan for the children to attend separate activities, thus allowing them time away from each other to pursue individual interests. Too many hours together, the family has learned, lead to increased tension and quarrels.

Other parents, who are not able to send their child to summer camps or relatives, make up a weekly schedule that varies the child's activities as much as possible. This schedule should provide for a consistent routine, physical activity, time for socializing with friends, and time away from brothers and sisters.

Here is a sample schedule for a thirteen-year-old girl in summer self-care:

	Day One	Day Two
10 AM	eat breakfast	eat breakfast
11 AM	home chores	home chores
12 PM	free time, TV	tennis lesson
1 PM	lunch	lunch
2 PM	swim (with sister)	friend's house (one child)
3 PM	free time, TV	errand at grocery store
6 PM	help with dinner	dinner

Each day is a variation of this schedule.

Activities such as baby-sitting, bowling, and reading, can be alternated while breakfast, lunch, and dinner occur at the same time each day.

These activities can be changed every four to six weeks, again maintaining stability but adding variety to the child's schedule. Chores can be an important part of the schedule, teaching a child responsibility and providing a source of rewards such as an allowance or special privileges.

"One of the things I learned," said a mother, "is that you have to expect—demand—that your child do something besides watch TV. I know that my son would have watched television all day every day even though he was bored to death. It would have been easier for me to let him; but that's not healthy!"

The same rule applies to daily visits to shopping centers, which may offer opportunities to be with friends but little in the way of constructive learning activities.

The Telephone

Many summer self-care plans include a provision that children let parents know, at all times, where they are. These messages are relayed through phone calls and notes. When possible, parents call once or twice a day just to check in. Some parents are fortunate enough to be able to eat lunch at home several times a week.

"Those are important calls," one child shared. "It's just nice to know that someone cares and is looking out for you. It also keeps us responsible; we have to be where we're supposed to be when Mom calls."

Transportation

One of the most difficult problems faced by parents designing a summer self-care plan is lack of transportation. This often requires innovative solutions.

Some parents barter such services. One parent was able to trade her child's baby-sitting services once a week for a free ride to the swimming pool. Other parents agreed to watch a neighbor's child during weekend hours in trade for weekday rides. However, many parents find that they have to hire transportation services for their children, some on a daily basis. Others have been able to pool resources and hire teenagers to drive their children.

Brothers and Sisters

Being in charge of brothers and sisters in the summer presents many special concerns when the summer hours are long. Ideally, if more than one child is home in the summer, each child can be home alone for short periods of time without supervision. However, when one child must supervise a younger child for more than forty hours a week, the child in charge has little or no time for his or her own interests and entertainment.

If one child is younger and needs constant supervision, parents should find ways to decrease the hours that an older child must be in charge. One parent we talked with said, "I've planned to send my youngest child to a day-care program every morning so that my oldest daughter will be able to take swimming lessons and visit friends. I just felt that watching her brother all week was not fair."

Even when each child is able to care for himself or herself, the fighting often intensifies when the children spend a lot of time together.

"Our challenge is more than just meeting each child's needs," shared one parent, "we also have to try to minimize the conflict between the two." When planning for summer self-care, be sure to review Chapter Eleven, "Brothers and Sisters."

Visitors

While visitors in the home are discussed in other parts of this book, a special emphasis is placed on finding ways that children may have contact with friends in the summertime. The most frequent complaint made by children in self-care is being unable to see friends.

"We talked about friends," said one parent. "The children felt that they shouldn't be punished and not allowed to see their friends just because we are not at home." Restricting children from seeing friends all summer can lead to bitter resentment of parents and rules by young teens.

Rules used by parents who choose to allow friends to visit include:

- Only during times scheduled in advance
- One friend in the house at a time
- Friends are not allowed in the house but may play outside

In some situations, parents may feel it unwise to allow friends in the house. Then, special care must be taken to see that their children have social activities outside the home, in the evenings, and on the weekends.

The Neighborhood

Some neighborhoods, because they are less safe or have no transportation, restrict the mobility of the child in self-care. Under such circumstances, a parent needs to be even more creative in meeting the needs of the child in summer self-care.

Frequently, resources outside the neighborhood, such as summer camps or activities close to a parent's job may be more appropriate even if it requires a child to be away from home all day.

One parent designed a weekly plan that included a morning activity close to where the parent worked, lunch with the parent, and a quick trip home where the child spent the rest of the afternoon. Another parent, concerned with the safety of her daughters, hired an older teenager to serve as a companion for the girls, ages twelve and thirteen. The companion walked the girls to the local park and gave them basketball lessons two afternoons a week. Both children were receptive to being taught sports but did not want a teenage baby-sitter.

ARE SUMMER SELF-CARE PLANS SAFE?

Some national experts say "no." Others say that it depends on the individual family and child. All say plans must be made carefully and reviewed periodically.

Once you and your child have designed a summer self-care plan, review it carefully. Are these plans arranged in a way that meets the developmental needs of adolescence? Of childhood? Is your child overloaded with responsibility? This is not the place to cut back on expenses; children need to feel safe and productive.

Good summer self-care plans involve an emotional as well as financial investment on the part of the parent. As with any self-care plan, you must be prepared to monitor your child regularly and carefully; this includes checking on home schedules that may change daily. You will find yourself continually teaching your child new skills, and you must be prepared to maintain an ongoing discussion with each child that will provide information enriching the summer self-care experience.

14

IS MY CHILD READY?

The decision to leave a child home alone in self-care is one of the most difficult decisions facing the working parent today. Whatever the pressures on the family to place a child in self-care, a parent must establish the same standards for that self-care situation that would be expected from any formal day-care program. These standards must include care that will meet a child's safety, social, educational, and recreational needs.

Obviously, a child cannot provide the same care that another adult can provide, but the issue is to be sure that the child will be able to care for himself or herself in a manner that will meet minimum physical and emotional needs.

WHEN IS YOUR CHILD READY FOR SELF-CARE?

The unfortunate fact is this: no one has discovered a magical age at which you can be sure that a child will be safe alone. Although day-care centers report that almost all children stop attending by age eleven or twelve, every child is different. Many children are not ready to assume responsibility for themselves at age twelve. Few children are ready before the ages of nine or ten.

Thus, careful evaluation of self-care as a day-care option for your child is imperative. Children placed in self-care before they are sufficiently capable of managing the responsibilities can be hurt—physically or emotionally—by the experience.

Several factors can help a parent decide if a child is ready for self-care. These include:

- The level of a child's skills and abilities
- The quality of the parent-child relationship
- The demands of the self-care plan
- The safety of the home and neighborhood

Each of these factors must be evaluated carefully.

Self-care is a very serious family decision; one that will ask the child or children involved to act as adults by behaving responsibly when there are problems, by making decisions that will affect the physical and emotional well-being of a child or children, by being able to discuss problems frankly that may be very troubling, by parenting a younger or less responsible brother or sister.

HOW TO EVALUATE YOUR CHILD'S ABILITIES FOR SELF-CARE

First, look carefully at the preceding chapters in this book; particularly those in the sections discussing emotional health and physical safety. These chapters establish minimal requirements for all good self-care plans. With those requirements in mind, the assessment provided here gains in scope and importance.

The best indicator of how prepared your child is for self-care is past performance in carrying out home responsibilities.

To determine this, ask yourself the following questions:

1. Does my child complete tasks according to directions?

The child who follows through with daily responsibilities—chores, home rules, and schoolwork—shows a willingness and a readiness to be responsible. On the other hand, a child who needs constant reminders, reprimands, or does not complete jobs may not be ready for self-care.

Being responsible also means that tasks are completed according to expectations and within a specific time frame. Thus, a parent considering self-care should ask the following: Does my child return home from school on time? Does he or she let me know where he or she is going? When he or she is coming home? Does my child do chores in a manner that meets my expectations?

2. Does my child communicate well? Does he or she bring up problems that occur in self-care?

Good communication between parent and child is essential for any successful self-care plan. Under the best of circumstances, children often do not like to report problems to their parents. Some may not even recognize potentially dangerous situations. If your child does not regularly discuss problems with you, whether school- or home-related, it is unlikely that problems in self-care will be communicated.

3. Does my child generally use good judgment?

Self-care requires a child to be capable of resolving problems. Ask yourself these questions: Does my child recognize alternatives when dealing with problems? Is he or she easily frustrated? Does my child usually find a solution with which I am also comfortable? Does my child hesitate to ask for help or advice?

These factors are all important in making good decisions, especially in a potentially dangerous situation.

In making a decision to leave your child home alone, consider very carefully how much difficulty your child experiences solving problems.

4. Do others see my child as responsible?

Ask people who know your child—grandparents, friends, parents of your child's friends, teachers. These people may provide a more objective assessment. They may also have suggestions for strengthening your child's skills.

5. What will self-care require of my child?

Every self-care plan will be unique—tailored to the individual family. Chapter Fifteen of this book, "How to Design Your Self-Care Plan," describes how to set up a self-care plan for your child. Once you have completed such a plan, reevaluate your child's ability to carry out the responsibilities. Are the hours too long? Will he or she have enough time with parents? With friends? For recreation and school activities?

Not only is it important to evaluate the self-care plan, but also the dangers that may exist for your child in your neighborhood.

Is your neighborhood relatively safe, or do you fear that your child could be physically harmed? Are other children in the neighborhood supervised? Do they tend to get into trouble? Are there neighbors, friends, or relatives nearby?

Evaluate your home environment. Have you inspected your home for possible health or fire hazards?

EMOTIONAL READINESS

If your answers to the preceding questions are positive, your child may have the skills necessary for self-care. However, one more issue is equally important: emotional readiness.

To assess this, ask yourself the following questions: Does my child have a short attention span? Require a great deal of attention? Need to be around people most of the time? Tend to be easily frightened?

If the answer to these questions is "yes," your child may require more direction, support, and contact with people than many self-care plans provide. If "no," then proceed with this evaluation of your child.

What Is the Quality of My Relationship with My Child?

The relationship between a parent and a child greatly influences how successful a self-care plan will be. When parent-child relationships are positive, children usually do well in self-care. In parent-child relationships where there is conflict and tension, children often behave poorly when unsupervised. They are a risk to themselves and to other children.

Evaluate your relationship with your child: Is your relationship supportive, with both of you getting along well? Do you talk easily and frequently? Have fun together?

Do outside pressures make your relationship one that is characterized by fights? Lack of communication? Disciplinary problems at home or at school?

Consider also the emotional support that you can provide to the child home alone. Are you available by phone? Can you be home in a short period of time? Do you work many miles away? Are there neighbors and friends who can provide support when you are not available?

How Does My Child Feel About Self-Care?

Have a thorough discussion with your child about how he or she feels about being alone. It may be a discussion that will take place over an extended period of time in order to be sure you have given your child plenty of opportunity to bring up any worries.

Start by asking your child how he or she feels about taking full responsibility for self-care—safety, meals, chores, dealing with strangers. What appeals to your child about self-care? What will be missed most from the present day-care arrangement? Does your child resist talking about being home alone? Why? What does your child think will help most to make self-care safe?

IS MY CHILD READY FOR SELF-CARE?

Now work with your child to complete the following by placing a check in front of those areas in which you feel your child may encounter problems:

1. Does my child carry out responsibilities according to my directions? Follow home rules? Tell me where he or she is?
2. Does my child generally use good judgment?
3. Do we have a good relationship?
4. Does my child tell me about problems he or she has at school? At home? When alone?
5. Does my child know and practice personal safety and first-aid skills?
6. Have we run through a mock fire hazard, a health problem, a stranger on the phone or at the door?
7. Has our house been inspected recently for health and safety hazards?
8. Is our neighborhood considered safe?
9. Can my child reach me easily by phone?
10. Are all aspects of our self-care plan acceptable to all family members?
11. Do I have adequate parental and other adult support for my child?
12. Do others consider my child responsible?
13. Does my child feel good—safe—in self-care?

Self-Care Checklist

Begin a checklist of problems that you feel your child might encounter. Such a list can be drawn from the evaluation form you have just completed, and can serve as an outline for the critically important discussion that must be an ongoing feature of any self-care plan.

THE SELF-CARE TEST

Now is the time to assess your child's ability to care for himself or herself. This is done by leaving your child alone for increasingly longer intervals; always with directions to be followed in your absence.

For example, leave your child for two hours with the following directions: "Please don't leave the house until I return. If anything comes up, call me at Mr. Jones's house."

This gives you an opportunity to see if your child will follow directions. Continue this testing by leaving your child for longer periods of time while increasing the number of instructions.

After you have done this several times, sit down with your child and talk about these experiences. How did he or she feel about being home alone?

If your child seems to adjust successfully to these arrangements, extend the test by increasing the time you leave on a regular basis: for example, three times a week for three hours each time.

Continue talking with your child about his or her feelings and continue to evaluate the child's actions during the time you are gone.

Most important, be honest with yourself about how your child is really doing in self-care. In our experience, many parents may decide that a child will be all right in self-care although there are signs of potential problems. Even if your day-care options are limited, you must be realistic about your child's performance in self-care.

IS MY CHILD READY FOR
SELF-CARE WITH SIBLINGS?

As the preceding test is only an indicator of how well a child may do in caring for himself or herself, being home with brothers and sisters introduces new problems that demand additional skills.

Ideally, any child would have an opportunity to test skills in caring for himself or herself before caring for brothers and sisters.

If you are considering leaving a young child at home, you should also plan to evaluate your older child's readiness and ability to assume that responsibility.

Consider carefully the following:

How well is each child able to assume the responsibilities of self-care?

Generally, children who are close in age or who are both able to care for themselves do not do well in self-care when one child is made responsible for another. Such situations work much better when each child is responsible for himself or herself. This means that each child must be evaluated independently of the other.

How well can the older child supervise a younger brother and sister in self-care?

If one child in a family is much younger and needs supervision, you must evaluate your older child's abilities to care for a child so young. One effective way to test this is to offer problems requiring the oldest child to make decisions about the care of the younger child. These should include examples in which the older child must respond to a child who will not follow the rules, who is fearful, who has a minor injury, and who does not come home after school.

Keep in mind that children will frequently know the correct responses but will choose to respond in a punitive manner to a younger brother or sister. Watch and listen for signs that tell you how younger children are being supervised. (Chapter Eleven, "Brothers and Sisters," describes potential problems faced by brothers and sisters home alone.)

Does your older child have the ability and desire to solve these problems appropriately? Can your child empathize with the feelings of younger brothers and sisters? Parents report that most children do not acquire these complex skills until at least age eleven or twelve. For safety's sake, do not underestimate the demands likely to be made on your older child.

How Well Do Your Children Get Along?

While some fighting and disagreements between brothers and sisters are normal, healthy, and a part of the maturing process, it is important to assess your children's abilities to resolve conflicts between them. Is every disagreement a replay of World War II? Do your children exhibit some ability to solve their problems without your interference or direction? Are there times when your children do help and support each other?

A parent should be especially sensitive in using self-care in a newly formed stepfamily. For example, an older child supervising new stepbrothers or stepsisters may find that they will not take direction from someone who is "not my 'real' brother or sister." Beginning a self-care arrangement too quickly may only increase initial tensions that most blended families experience in living together.

In any family where self-care experiences increase tensions among children, it is usually best to separate children who do not get along.

Do Any of Your Children Require Special Care Skills?

You must make the same careful evaluation anytime an older child will be responsible for the care of a physically or mentally disabled brother or sister. In such care arrangements, assess not only your child's ability to care for a brother or sister with special needs, but also evaluate the child's ability to cope with the stress that is often a part of caring for such a child.

AM I READY FOR SELF-CARE?

The decision to place a child in self-care demands that parents honestly question if they themselves are ready for self-care. A good self-care plan requires rigorous parental involvement: parents must regularly monitor the child in the home, continue to teach the child new skills, and maintain an ongoing dialogue in order to address a child's feelings and problems in self-care. This requires a lot of time and energy, especially after a long day's work.

Ask yourself the following questions:

- Am I ready to make the commitment of time and supervision that will make this a constructive, supportive experience for my child?
- Am I comfortable with my assessment of my child's skills and abilities?
- Am I anxious about leaving my child in self-care?

Consider how your child passed the "self-care test." Consider too the responsibilities outlined for both parent and child in self-care. Leaf through this book and the chapters that deal with physical safety and emotional health.

If your child seems unable or unwilling to be in self-care, please consider other forms of day-care or supervised activity. *Don't risk harm to your child.*

You should not feel that this is the final answer if your child is not ready. Kids mature at different rates, and six months from now your child may pass the "self-care test" with flying colors. Remember, emotional readiness is as important as your child's ability to physically care for himself or herself.

As a final step in assessing your child's readiness, turn the book over to your child. The final chapter, "For Kids Only," is an introduction to the experiences that other children have had in self-care, written for children. This chapter can provide your child with a fairly accurate picture of the self-care experience.

15

HOW TO DESIGN YOUR SELF-CARE PLAN

If you and your child have decided that self-care is workable for your family, now is the time to write down the house rules, a contract, and other agreements that will be essential to the success of your self-care plan.

Families consistently tell us that taking this time with children to formulate and write a detailed family self-care plan has cleared up many misunderstandings. The rules, the contract, and the agreements that make up the self-care plan then become the standards by which you are able to judge the success of your child's performance in self-care—a set of clearly written measures.

This chapter begins with house rules, the cornerstone of a self-care plan. We then look at family self-care contracts. Carefully read each section before completing the family self-care contract.

You will want to review other sections of this book, such as the chapters on brothers and sisters or young teens, in which you may have already established some rules or agreements, and include these in your contract.

HOUSE RULES

All children respond best in structured situations where they understand exactly what is expected of them. Establishing house rules is the first step towards providing that structure.

Generally, families find that simplicity is the key. Establish just three or four basic rules that remind children of daily responsibilities such as chores and planned activities.

Here is an example taken from a note taped to a working mother's refrigerator in a home where the children are ages eleven and fourteen.

Our Care Rules

1. Phone me as soon as you get home from school. If I'm in a meeting, I'll call back as soon as I can.
2. All your tasks must be done by 6 PM or no TV! And I mean that, Jonathon. Now take a quick look at the chore chart to be sure you didn't forget if this is your week for a new job.
3. Clean up any food and dishes used for treats. That means you, Nicole. If you decide to make chocolate chip cookies, then I don't expect to have to wash the bowl. Fair?
4. If you decide to go somewhere, please leave a note telling me where you are and what time you'll be home. A phone call will also be appreciated if you'll be gone more than an hour.

   For your care and because I care!!
   Mom
P.S. Today's secret message is: Guess what happens Saturday?

The parents in this family like to leave a new message each morning after the children leave for school as a special welcome home to the empty house, and because they have found it a good way to ensure that their kids always take a quick peek at the all-important care rules.

As you can see, these rules help to remind the children what is expected of them when they are home alone. However, parents need to be even more specific in defining each child's role. What are the chores? How are they to be done?

For example, if Jack is responsible for cleaning up the breakfast dishes, he should know exactly how that is to be done. Does he wash them or simply stack them in the sink? Is he expected to wash, dry, and put dishes back on the shelf?

Walk through the steps of each chore with your child; this is an excellent way for a parent to be very clear about expectations. It is also a good way to know if a child is able to complete the task. This helps avoid frustration and feelings of failure if a child should be unable to perform a particular chore.

GUIDELINES FOR SETTING YOUR OWN HOUSE RULES

Be Positive

Always state your rules in positive terms. Rules that start with "don't" can make a child feel negative and rebellious. Use phrases such as "if you go out, then . . ." rather than "don't go out."

Establish Consequences

House rules are effective only if they can be enforced. This means that each rule should have a consequence that will encourage a child to carry out the responsibility. Remember that positive consequences are just as effective as negative ones. Carefully consider the rewards that will be built into the house rules as well as the penalties. Ask your child to suggest rewards and penalties.

Parents should check each day to see if rules are being followed. This is not only a check but also a way to communicate to your child that you are interested and ready to listen.

If you find that chores or other responsibilities have not been completed, then clearly understood consequences should be enforced. For example, if Susan forgot to put away her cheese and cracker snack, she should be asked to do so immediately, even though Mom is now home. It may also mean that Susan will lose some TV privileges that evening.

Be aware, too, that some rules are always going to be difficult to enforce. As children often do not report their own misbehavior, or deny it if someone else reports it, parents are then in the tough spot of judging behavior that they haven't actually seen.

Neighbors Can Help

Situations such as these can be more easily handled if you can ask a neighbor or friend or relative to assist with checking for serious violations of self-care rules. At the same time, your child should be fully aware of the request you have made of another adult. In fact, it might be very good to discuss with your child which adults are trusted and can be helpful to the family.

Always explain why a particular rule—whether it concerns leaving the yard or having friends in the house when no one is home—is so important that it merits an extra check.

If your child understands your concern and is encouraged to see another adult as a helpful resource and someone to turn to for help, you can avoid feelings of resentment or feeling spied on.

Also, a careful watch for strangers is necessary for safe self-care. This alone is an excellent reason for asking a neighbor to "keep an eye out."

Special Note: Remember, you are the parent and have a responsibility to ensure that your child is safe in self-care. Young teens may resent having neighbors report misbehavior. However, they have the choice of not breaking the rules or trying to renegotiate those they feel are unfair.

Before asking a neighbor, relative, or friend to check on your child, be sure that you discuss every aspect with your child—the rule that concerns you and why, the adult to be chosen, and how your child feels about that person.

Self-care is an expression of confidence in your child. Solutions to problems should be a joint concern of all family members, and should reflect love, not suspicion. If solutions do not work and you find that house rules are consistently violated, you may have a situation in which self-care may not be workable.

House Rules Can Measure the Effectiveness of Self-Care

As we stated earlier, house rules are yardsticks by which to measure the performance of your child in self-care. If you find that these rules are being broken regularly, assess the potential harm of those particular rules. Leaving dirty dishes may be irritating but it certainly won't affect the physical or emotional health of your child. On the other hand, leaving the house for long periods of time without permission suggests a serious rule violation. This, as we said, may force you to reconsider self-care.

House Rules Need Prominent Posting

When you and your child have settled on your house rules, post them in a prominent place. Some families use a simple card with large lettering, and attach the card to the refrigerator or family bulletin board.

One family decided to tape a large poster to the back door. This poster had *two* sets of house rules—one for the kids, and one for their working parents! Mom's and Dad's rules included making regular phone calls to the house, seeing that certain snack foods were always in the cupboard, and writing their weekly work schedules on the family calendar. The kids had a good time helping to establish the parent's house rules.

THE FAMILY SELF-CARE CONTRACT

House rules work to remind children of some of the responsibilities expected of them if they are going to be home alone in self-care. However, a more comprehensive outline of self-care is needed in order to define fully a family's self-care plan.

We call this outline the "Family Self-Care Contract."

Here is an example of a family contract that has been used to set rules, establish guidelines, and adapt the plan to a family's special needs. Please look it over and read the suggestions that follow before trying to set up your own contract.

Family Self-Care Contract

This is an agreement of all members of our family to follow these self-care rules. We will review our contract every six months and when problems arise.

1. Play Rules:

Where you may play:

Whom you may play with when your parents are not at home:

What you should tell parents about your play plans, including where, when, and how much they need to know about your activities:

2. Phone rules:

Always answer the phone in the following manner:

Check in every day with Mom or Dad:

The following situations require a phone call to a parent:

For which emergencies will you call a parent first? Which parent will you call? For which emergencies will you call 911 or the police first?

Home phone privileges and other rules include:

(Be sure to read Chapter Five, "Physical Safety.")

3. Home chores:

Time limits:

Rewards and Consequences:

4. Care of Brothers and Sisters:

Who is in charge? If an older child is in charge, list specific responsibilities:

List the responsibilities of the other children:

5. Discipline:

Who will be disciplining other children?

Who decides when discipline is necessary? What happens then?

What type of discipline is appropriate?

Emergency Procedures

In case of physical injury:

Fire:

Poison:

Be sure to read and complete the exercises on physical safety in Chapters Five through Ten.
Other agreements:

Signed By:

Parent _____

Parent _____

Child _____

Child _____

GUIDELINES FOR WRITING
YOUR SELF-CARE CONTRACT

Before you and your child sit down to write your family's self-care contract, spend time discussing everyone's ideas and feelings based on the special circumstances facing your family. Review the chapters in this book that focus on the emotional and physical well-being of your child. This will help you organize your thoughts and ensure that you have covered a number of key points and issues.

Take your time. The more you review before actually writing your contract, the easier it will be to complete a contract with your child. Be sure that your child also reviews these sections of the book, especially the sections on physical safety, and Chapter Sixteen, "For Kids Only."

Plan a period of time when you and your child can sit down together and discuss each potential rule. Actively seek your child's opinions. Discuss each point and listen for both the physical as well as the emotional needs that your child expresses. Learn to listen between the lines.

For example, if your child is adamant that he or she have time for contact with friends each day, be aware that your child is likely to feel lonely. Some children need much more social time than others, and the balance between time spent alone and with friends can be one of those elements that makes self-care work well for the entire family.

Plan Talk Time

These discussions don't just happen; you have to plan for them. We recommend that you plan a family meeting to discuss the agreements that will structure your self-care plan. Use the sample self-care contract to guide your discussion. Once your agreements are established, they must be reviewed regularly, and those reviews planned for.

The following suggestions have been helpful for many families:

1. **Family meetings:** Family members meet every three months to discuss changes in the contract. Always pick a time and a date for the next meeting.

2. **Informal discussions:** Establish a time that parent and child will be available each night for discussion of problems as well as the good things that happened that day. Remember, before dinner is a hectic time for most families. When you listen—really listen.

When You and Your Child Find It Difficult to Talk

When children are unwilling to discuss self-care rules, try to determine why. Is your child telling you that he or she does not want to stay home alone? Is your child a young teen who speaks in short sentences and does not like any rules that restrict freedom?

Also, it helps to work together to draw up a list of all the options relating to the rule under discussion without evaluating any particular one. Be as creative as the situation will allow. Review each option and evaluate its potential benefits and consequences. With younger children, try to offer three choices for evaluation.

Be aware of the children's emotional needs as well as your need for assurance that they are well protected in terms of physical safety. Perhaps you can give a little on your side if the children are willing to compromise through extra phone calls or whatever is needed to make you feel good about the final solution.

Special Note: Children are more likely to follow through with agreements and assume responsibilities when they feel that they have been involved in the process—participants in every step of the development of your family's self-care plan.

SAMPLES OF OTHER FAMILIES' SELF-CARE CONTRACTS

As we mentioned earlier, each family's self-care plan will be unique, designed specifically for the needs of the child and the needs of the parents. Each will reflect the age of the child, the neighborhood in which the family lives, and the special circumstances relating to each parent.

The following examples are family self-care contracts drawn up by parents and children who have experienced self-care as a family effort.

The Miller Family

This contract was written by Rich and Sharon Miller with the help of their son, Dusty, age nine.

---

1. Play rules:

   No friends will play inside our house if Mom and Dad are not home.

   Every Monday after school I will go straight to Peter's house for Cub Scouts and stay there until Dad picks me up.

   Every Wednesday after school I will go home with Sarah and stay at her house until Dad picks me up.

   I will always call Mom to tell her I have arrived home or that I am at Peter's or Sarah's house.

2. Phone calls:

   Mom and Dad will always call me with a secret ring. They will ring once, hang up, then call back and let the phone ring four times before I'll answer it.

   I will always call Mom if there is an emergency with the house or with me.

   I will not use any first aid without calling her first.

   If I start to feel scared, first I'll watch TV for a little while to see if the feeling goes away. If I still feel scared, then I'll call Mom or Dad.

   If I feel lonely, I'll tell myself to play a game or read or find something to do. If I feel lonely a lot, I will tell Mom or Dad.

   Every day I must call Mom when I get home from school.

3. Stranger Rules:

   I never answer the door for anyone.

   If I see a stranger in our yard, I will call Mom immediately.

   If someone tries to come into our house, I will call the police by dialing 911.

4. Home Chores:

   Every day I will clean and wipe off the kitchen table. This means I will clear the dishes and stack them neatly. Then I'll use a clean dishcloth to wipe the table and I'll be sure to rinse it out.

Dad will check my work.

Mom and Dad will pay me $2.00 a week for doing my job.

5. Emergency Procedures:

In case of fire, I'll leave the house, go to the Smiths, and call the fire department; then I'll call Mom and Dad.

If I'm not sure about how badly I might be hurt, I'll call Mom.

Signed	Rich Miller, Father
	Sharon Miller, Mother
	Dusty Miller, Son
Date	March 27th

You can see that the Miller's contract reflects a family's concern for a young child. Dusty is restricted in phone and play privileges according to his ability to handle these responsibilities.

As both his parents feel that their neighborhood is fairly safe, Dusty is allowed to visit friends once a week.

Dusty is an only child. For this reason, his parents have agreed to make a special effort to compensate for the time he spends alone. They never leave him for more than two hours each weekday as they feel this is the maximum time he should spend in self-care.

The Brown Family

This contract was written by Mrs. Brown, a single working parent, with daughter Susie, age eleven, and son Tom, age nine. Mrs. Brown is allowed to use a telephone only during break time at the plant where she is employed.

1. Play rules:

We agree that no other children will be allowed to play in our apartment while we are here by ourselves.

We agree that we will not leave the apartment to play outside.

If we wish to play with a friend, we must tell Mother two days ahead of time so she can make the arrangements.

We must talk with Mother at 3:30 every afternoon so she knows we have arrived at our apartment or friend's apartment safely.

The friend must be someone in this building or someone riding the bus so that we are not outside alone except for when we get off the school bus to enter the building.

2. Phone calls:

We can answer the phone but we must never let anyone think that we are here alone.

We cannot be on the phone between 3:25 and 3:45 so that Mother can call us during her break. We should both be here.

If one of us does not get home on time for any reason, the other is to call Mrs. Jones or go downstairs to knock on her door.

If one of us misses the school bus, we must call Mrs. Jones so she can tell the other what happened.

If there is any emergency we should call Mother by asking for Mr. Gray, her supervisor.

Each of us can call friends after school, but no call should last longer than fifteen minutes.

3. Strangers:

We can answer the door by checking the peephole and asking who is there, but the door is to remain locked at all times. No one is allowed to come in unless Mother says that it is okay. If it is important, we can call her by asking for Mr. Gray and telling him that it is an emergency call.

If Mother knows someone is going to come over, she will let us know the day before or call us or Mrs. Jones.

4. Home Chores:

Susie picks up the living room.

Tom sweeps the kitchen floor.

Susie will fix one cold meal each week.

Tom will set the table every evening.

All chores are to be done by 6 P.M.

Mother will pay us our allowance every Friday.

5. Care of brother and sister:

Neither of us is in charge of the other. We are each responsible for our own actions. Neither of us should discipline the other.

If one of us breaks a rule, does not come home on time, or leaves without permission, the other should tell Mother when she gets home from work, unless it is an emergency. An emergency is not coming home or leaving without permission.

We must remember that Mother really shouldn't answer the phone except during her breaks.

6. Emergencies:

If there is a fire in our apartment or in our building, we should go stay with Mrs. Jones. If the fire is in our apartment, we should pull the alarm in the hall as we run to Mrs. Jones's apartment, then call the fire department.

If we are ever hurt, we should go immediately to Mrs. Jones. She can help us with first aid. If we cannot do that, we should call Mother right away. We can tell Mr. Gray it is an emergency. We can also call 911 if it is very bad.

If Mrs. Jones can't help us, we should call Mr. Woodward, our superintendent.

Signed	Mary Brown, Mother
	Susie Brown, Daughter
	Tom Brown, Son
Date	July 13th

The Brown family contract shows the special concerns of a family with two children home alone. Because the children are close in age, Mrs. Brown decided that each child will be responsible for his or her own care.

One special feature of this self-care contract is the restriction on outside play. Mrs. Brown worries about the safety of her neighborhood, especially for children the ages of Susie and Tom. To compensate for the time they must spend indoors, she has allowed them more extensive phone privileges so they have other ways of staying in contact with friends.

She also makes it a point to spend time several evenings a week at either the local shopping center, or a nearby, well-lit park, so that the children have a chance to release some of their harnessed energy and play with friends.

YOUR FAMILY'S SELF-CARE CONTRACT

Now, complete your own family's self-care contract. This contract will be invaluable in helping each family member understand what is needed to make self-care work for you and your child.

Self-care contracts cannot, however, ensure that a child will do well in self-care. A child may or may not be able to follow agreements made within the contract. Younger children may not have the abilities, self-control, or problem-solving skills to perform successfully in self-care. Older children may choose not to follow many of the rules. No self-care plan can anticipate all the problems; difficulties will arise that are not clearly defined within the self-care plan.

Consider the family self-care contract to be a working agreement—one that will need close monitoring and revisions on a regular basis. Is your child able to follow all the rules in the family contract? Do agreements or rules need changing? Even the best self-care plan will require revisions on a regular basis. Schedules will change, abilities will change, and rules will change.

FAMILY CALENDAR

Self-care will work best for everyone in your family if you all make an extra effort to talk regularly about those parts of your self-care plan that are working well, and those that are not.

In order to help you do that, we suggest that you mark the following on your family calendar as reminders to check these parts of your family self-care plan.

Every three months, check:

- First-Aid Kit—Do you need any new supplies?
- First-Aid Procedures—Give your child a quick quiz on cuts and burns.
- Home Emergency Kit—Do you need new batteries? Are your fire extinguishers in working order?
- Home Emergency Procedure—Run through turning off the water and electricity.
- Emergency Phone Numbers—Have any changed?
- Safety People—Have the people whom your child can call in an emergency changed? Is your work situation different? Can you always be easily reached by telephone? Does your child know whom to call first—Mom or Dad?
- Do you have medical releases with all the safety people? Do you need to get more to anyone?
- Hold a family fire drill.

- Practice two different kinds of emergency phone calls—one to you, and one to the police or 911.

Every six months, check:

- Your Self-Care Agreement: Have a family conference to go over all parts in case some need reassessment or change.
- Family Chores: Is it time to change these in order to add variety to your child's day? Is he or she willing to do more? Have you overloaded your child?
- Physical Safety Exercises: Review your child's completed exercises. What continues to worry your child in your home? Your neighborhood?
- Emotional Health: Look at these chapters and, as a family, discuss how your child feels today about self-care. Does your child have strong feelings of fear, loneliness, or boredom? Is your child sharing these feelings with you easily and frequently? Do you need to try some new ways to communicate?
- Activities: Is it time to find new activities for your child during the self-care hours? Can you find new ways to spend time with your child?
- Conferences: If you do not have regular school conferences to discuss your child's performance, this will be a good time to do so. If your child is having serious problems with self-care, you may find that this is reflected in schoolwork and activity.

Are there other parts of your self-care plan that you feel need regular checking? If so, list them here as a reminder:

16

FOR KIDS ONLY

This chapter is about how kids in self-care feel about this experience. The following remarks were made during classes designed to teach self-care. We always ask kids to tell us how they feel about it. Some really like it; they like getting to make their own decisions when their parents are not home.

Others hate self-care. They miss their friends. Some dislike taking care of their brothers or sisters. Some boys and girls feel cheated because their parents work. Some children like self-care part of the time, but feel lonely or bored at other times.

Several children have told us that they pretend to like self-care when, in fact, they are very unhappy. Why do they pretend to like it? Most of them do not want to worry their Mom or Dad. They say that their parents already have too much to worry about, and their unhappiness would only make things worse.

Perhaps that's not the best thing to do. This chapter offers you some advice about ways in which you can help yourself feel better about self-care. Some of these suggestions may be just what you need, others may not interest you. You may feel very good about being in self-care, but may want to read about other children's feelings and some of the problems they have.

TALKING STRAIGHT

We tell children in class that they need to "talk straight" with their parents. Holding your feelings in—not telling anyone how you feel—when you really dislike being home alone is not healthy for you. Your parents cannot help you feel better about self-care unless you talk about things as they really are. Your parents probably gave you this book to read because they care how you feel.

We know that sometimes you want to talk straight with your parents but you don't know what to say. Some of you may find talking straight difficult because many families just don't talk much about feelings and problems.

When you have a problem, the following suggestions may help you talk straight with your parents:

1. Tell them what you think the problem is.
2. Tell them how you feel; why it is important to you.
3. Say what you think would solve the problem.
4. Carefully pick your time to talk with your parents. Remember, parents are usually exhausted when they first come home from work. You and your parents should decide together on the best time for sharing problems.
5. Keep your temper, even if you don't get everything you want.
6. If it is difficult for you to talk with your parents, write down what you are thinking and feeling. Many of us find it much easier to put our problems on paper.

Talking straight can really make a difference. John, a twelve-year-old boy, was very unhappy about not seeing his friends after school. He told his parents about his feelings and said that he would really like to visit a friend two days a week after school.

To John's surprise, his parents agreed! They were happy to help him work this out. Two days weren't possible because of the family schedule, but John was able to visit a friend one day a week with an extra day from time to time.

FEELING FRIGHTENED

Children in our classes often talk about feeling frightened when they are home alone. Fear is a natural feeling that everyone has from time to time. In fact, fear can be a helpful feeling: it lets us know when things may be unsafe.

When you feel afraid, the first thing to do is decide if there is a real danger. Did you see a stranger peeking in your back window? If so, you *should* be afraid! Call a parent or the police.

On the other hand, did you hear a funny noise in the basement? That is something that is not likely to hurt you even though you still feel scared.

Each time you feel afraid, ask yourself: Is this something that I *know* is serious or is it something that scares me? Remind yourself that few children ever have dangerous experiences when they are home alone.

Here are some suggestions to help you feel less frightened. They have been made by other children who use them when *they* are alone and feeling frightened:

1. Inspect the house when you first come home. Check all those places that seem to have strange noises or scare you when it's dark or late.

2. Call a parent or a friend. Do you have some friends who are also in self-care? Maybe you could have a special "fright plan" to help each other feel better. Check to see if your community has PhoneFriend, people you can call for just this reason. Look at Chapter Five, "Physical Safety" for ways to use the telephone when you are frightened.

3. Turn up the television set to make yourself stop thinking about weird noises.

4. Play with a pet. This will take your mind off worries about yourself. You'll have fun instead of fear.

Sometimes children frighten themselves by watching scary movies on TV after school. Scary movies may be fun but they can leave you with a terrible feeling afterwards. If a movie really scares you, turn it off! You'll be glad later.

Now ask yourself these questions about your feelings in self-care. Answer each one honestly!

1. I get scared when . . .

2. I worry most about . . .

3. I feel safer if . . .

4. When I'm home alone, I feel scared . . . a little? a lot? never? . . .

Share these answers with your parents. Together you may be able to feel less afraid.

FEELING BORED

When we talk with children, many say that being home alone is boring because there's nothing to do except watch TV. Yet, other children aren't bored at all, and some are bored only part of the time.

What can you do when you are feeling bored? Tom, who is eleven years old, had that problem. He said that he felt very sad in self-care because there was nothing to do. We suggested that Tom—with the help of his classmates—make a list of things he could do at home by himself. Here it is:

- Read a book.
- Take the dog for a walk.
- Practice shooting baskets.
- Call a friend.
- Do a chore.
- Do homework.
- Write a story.
- Make an art project.
- Start a hobby; collect stamps.

As Tom and his classmates talked, they decided that being bored is really a choice that people make. Tom looked at his list and decided that at least part of the time he could choose not to mope around. He could *choose* to do something from his list.

Tom went home and tried several ideas, but he still felt bored at times. Tom had a self-care situation that was different from some of the other children's. His mom and dad were divorced, and his mom, with whom he lived, worked very long hours. She seldom got home before seven o'clock at night! Tom was indeed home alone for a long period of time.

"Tell your mom how you feel about being alone for such a long time," said one of the boys in the class.

Tom wasn't sure he wanted to to that. "My mom worries too much about me being home alone already," he said.

The children in the class insisted, "Tell your mom."

The next week Tom came to class feeling much better. "I told my mom about my feelings," he said. "She is going to have my dad pick me up at home two days a week at 5:30. The other three days I can use ideas from my list.

Two months later we talked with Tom again. He was feeling much better; his boredom had disappeared.

FEELING LONELY

Most children in our classes talk about missing their friends when they are in self-care. Older children—ages thirteen, fourteen, and fifteen—miss their friends even more than younger children do.

This is a natural feeling; even children whose parents are home after school say that they do not have enough time with their friends. If you feel lonely often, and have little or no time with friends, tell your parents. Here are some suggestions you can make that your parents might like:

1. Call a friend.
2. Join a club or group.
3. Take part in a school activity or sport.
4. Invite a friend over (with parents' approval).
5. Volunteer to help at a community hospital or organization.
6. Go to the library, park, community center, shopping center; perhaps do errands for Mom or Dad.
7. Play with my pet.

If your parents let you have friends over to visit, make sure that your friends know and follow your house rules. Talk with your parents about those friends you think will be able to follow the rules. Choose carefully; having friends over is a privilege that requires you to act responsibly. You don't want to lose this valuable privilege.

If your parents do not want you to have other children in the house, ask if you can go over to a friend's house, play outside, or have friends over on the weekends. Keep thinking of ideas until you and your parents can agree on something that will make you feel better.

SUMMERTIME AND LONELINESS

Summer can be an especially hard time to be alone a lot. Children in self-care for long periods of time often begin to feel very sad and depressed. One child, who was home almost all summer said, "I just felt awful all the time. I quit trying after a while because nothing seemed fun to do."

If you are going to be in self-care this summer, work hard with your parents to come up with a summer plan. Look for things to do all around you—at school, at church, in the library, the community center. Check hobby and computer stores for project ideas. Talk with your parents about all the possibilities. Sometimes parents never hear of things that might be fun to do. In fact, you may not like all the activities that you do, but remember, it is better than giving up and moping at home.

BROTHERS AND SISTERS

Many children in self-care have a brother or sister who stays with them. Having a brother or sister at home with you can make you feel good; it keeps you from getting lonely and bored. Other times, you may not feel so good; children who are the oldest often complain about having to watch over younger brothers or sisters who won't mind, while younger children complain of older brothers or sisters who ignore or mistreat them.

Here's some advice for you—whether you are a brother or a sister, the oldest or the youngest! Read the section written especially for you and see if the ideas might be helpful.

If You Are the Oldest Child

If you are the oldest in your family and are expected to care for your younger brothers and sisters, you have a big responsibility. Caring for younger children requires a lot of work! When the other children won't mind you, it can be very frustrating.

We hope that your parents have taught you what to do when you have problems. If they haven't, ask them each time you have a problem so that you can learn better ways to manage the younger children. Remember, little kids don't like to be bossed around by an older brother or sister. Sometimes you have to find clever ways to get them to do the right thing. Chapter Eleven, "Brothers and Sisters," has advice for you; be sure to read it!

To Tell or Not to Tell—What Is Tattling?

Being responsible for brothers and sisters means that you *do* tell parents when there are problems. Many times, the oldest child doesn't like to tell on brothers and sisters because that seems like tattling. It is tattling if you just want to get the other child in trouble or if the problem isn't serious.

For example, if your brother takes your baseball cap and you call your mom, that's tattling. However, if your brother leaves the yard without permission, you *should* tell your mom or dad. Your parents need to know when house rules are broken; that's being responsible.

Don't Be Mean

Some children really dislike taking care of a younger brother or sister. Karen, a thirteen-year-old girl in our class, had to take care of her younger sister each day. She hated having to be the baby-sitter! Pretty soon she found herself being mean to her little sister, even though the family's self-care plan wasn't the little sister's fault. Afterwards, she would feel guilty for being so angry and mean. When Karen's mom found out how she was treating her sister, Karen got in a lot of trouble. The best thing she could have done was to have told her parents just how she felt; perhaps then the situation could have been changed before all the bad feelings happened.

Getting Annoyed

Sometimes the oldest child does not have to care for a younger brother or sister, but is at home with him or her each day. Even when you are not responsible for their care, younger children can be annoying. Often, they want to be with you more than you want to be with them. They'll probably annoy you until you pay attention to them.

The best way to handle this problem is to spend *some* time with your brother or sister and then find time for yourself.

If You Are a Younger Child

Being in self-care with an older brother or sister can be fun, or it can be terrible. Some brothers and sisters like taking care of younger children while others do not. If your brother or sister is mean to you, it may be that he or she doesn't like having to care for someone else; it doesn't mean there's something wrong with you!

How can you get along better with an older brother or sister? Pay attention to what makes an older child mad. If your brother or sister doesn't like to spend time playing with you, find things to do by yourself. Remember, if you annoy other family members, they'll probably get angry.

Getting Teased

Some older brothers and sisters like to tease younger children. Bill, age nine, was always being teased by his older brother. The class told him to ignore what his brother said. Bill tried this. At first, his brother would tease him more. Finally, after days of being ignored, Bill's brother stopped the teasing. Bill did say, though, that it was really hard work ignoring all the teasing.

Your Rights

While older brothers or sisters may be mean to you, you do have certain rights. You should have the right to watch some of your television programs or to use the phone. You certainly have the right not to be hurt by an older brother or sister. If these rights are ignored, you should tell your mom or dad—even if your older brother or sister threatens to hurt you. Let your parents help you decide how to solve these problems.

One suggestion I have is that you make a list of your rights here, then discuss these with your parents and with the older children in the family. They should add their rights to this list, too.

Children's Rights

RULES

Remember that you are always responsible for following house rules when you are in self-care. Sometimes your older brother or sister may remind you of these rules in a rude way, by yelling at you, but you must still go by the rules. Your parents will not know *how* you were told, but they will know if you broke the rule. If rudeness is a problem between you and the older children, talk this over with your parents.

DISCIPLINE

You, your parents, and your brothers and sisters must decide how discipline will be handled in your family. If you feel that your brother (or sister) is too strict, or if you are being hurt, tell your parents. Try to understand how the older children feel, too. The better everyone understands one another, the more interesting and enjoyable self-care can be!

FOR ALL CHILDREN

Use these pages to make some lists that you should read from time to time. These lists can be very helpful in showing you how well you are doing in self-care.

Things I Enjoy the Most in Self-Care

Things I Don't Like About Self-Care

Things I Can Do When I'm Bored

Things I Can Do When I'm Lonely

Things I Can Do When I'm Scared

Reminders: Things I Should Talk Over with Mom and Dad

BIBLIOGRAPHY

Ames, Louise Bates, *He Hit Me First*. Dembner Books, New York, 1982.

Ginott, Dr. Haim G., *Between Parent and Teenager*. Avon Books, New York, 1971.

Kreidler, William, *Creative Conflict Resolution*. Scott, Foresman and Co., Glenview, Ill. 1984.

Kyte, Kathy S., *In Charge: A Complete Handbook for Kids with Working Parents*. Alfred A. Knopf, New York 1983.

Long, Lynette and Thomas, *The Handbook for Latchkey Children and Their Parents*. Arbor House, New York 1983.

Long, Lynette, *On My Own*, Acropolis Books Ltd., Washington, D.C. 1984.

Price, Jane, *How to Have a Child and Keep Your Job*. Penguin Books, New York 1980.

Schmitt, Dr. Barton D., *Pediatric Telephone Advice*. Little, Brown and Company, Boston 1980.

Schwarz, Meg, *TV and Teens*. Action For Children's Television, Addison-Wesley Publishing Co., Reading, Mass. 1982.

Sliwa, Curtis, *Street-Smart*. Addison-Wesley Publishing Co., Reading, Mass. 1982.

Swan, Helen L., Sherry Briggs and Mike Kelso, *I'm in Charge*. Johnson County Mental Health Center, Olathe, Kansas 1982.

Swan, Helen L., and Victoria Melcher Houston, *The Parent Guide Book*. Kansas Committee for the Prevention of Child Abuse, Topeka, Kansas 1983.

Index